ISBN: 1 971947 53 7
Published by

FERRY *Publications*

Ferry Publications Ltd, PO Box 9, Narberth,
Pembrokeshire, UK.
Tel: +44 (0) 1834 891460
Fax: +44 (0) 1834 891463

Greek
ferries
by John May

Contents

© All photographs by John May

Above: *The locally built **Paros** in the attractive harbour of Naxos in 1981.*

Overleaf Above: *An earlier generation of ferry in service in the early 1980s - the DFDS stalwart **Kronprinsesse Ingrid** served out her last years in Greek waters as the **Alkyon**. She is seen going astern in the Great Harbour at Piraeus at the start of a voyage to Rhodes in 1983.*

Overleaf Below: *The current generation of Greek ferries demonstrated by the **Superfast IV** accelerating away from Ancona on her 19 hour sailing to Patras in 1998.*

Introduction

When first travelling in Greece twenty years ago, the ferry ships then in service presented a splendid selection of elderly vessels from northern Europe, eking out their last years in the warm waters of the eastern Mediterranean. Regrettably, there was no accessible source of information at the time and many opportunities to see and to study the fascinating collection of vessels then in service were lost through ignorance of what was possible. Regular visits since then and extensive travelling around this most delightful of lands have developed a perception of a country which continues to confuse and fascinate in equal measure. While neither intended as a guide to travel in Greece nor as a history of the shipping companies operating ferry services in Greek waters, I hope that this book will add to the knowledge and understanding of a system which continues to produce surprising survivals from earlier eras and at the same time remarkably efficient demonstrations of the latest in shipping technology. It is a subject which is overdue for consideration outside Greece.

The scope of the book is to review how the Greek ferry system works, the companies currently participating in it and the over 300 ships in service in and around Greek waters. In some cases the companies also have operations elsewhere but these are ignored while, to achieve as comprehensive coverage as possible, ships are noted which regularly sail through Greek waters without actually calling at the ports of the country.

While many published sources have been consulted on the ships and services described, of which the most relevant are acknowledged at the end of the book, it derives to a very large extent from my own travels and reading on the spot and the photographs within were all taken by myself. Although the process of preparing the book has occupied a far longer period than my publishers had conceived possible, it cannot represent the last word on a subject which is changing so continuously and unpredictably.

John May

John May
September, 1999

Above: *Once fleet mates at Ostend and later rivals in the trade from Rafina, the **Bari Express** and **Superferry II** were originally Belgian Marine's **Prinsesse Astrid** and **Prince Laurent**..*

Part 1 - The Greek Ferry Scene

The Country

Situated at the south-eastern corner of Europe, Greece is separated from the economic and political heart of modern Europe by the political maelstrom of the Balkan states. Greatly influenced by the role of the sea in its history and current life, it is a country with a remarkable network of ferry services.

The land area of Greece is about the size of England but features a coastline of almost fifteen thousand kilometres, a third of that of the entire Mediterranean Sea. While much of the country is mountainous, making land communication an arduous exercise, no point on the Greek mainland is more than one hundred and fifty kilometres from the sea. Greece was the last country in Europe to take up railways and it has only been since Greece was admitted to the European Union in 1981 that the resulting inflow of subsidies and grant aid have seen the completion of the road network to all parts of the mainland and the improvement of motorways to a standard which has made the regular movement of freight by road a realistic possibility.

While the geography of Greece produces a country in which communication is difficult by road and fragmentary by rail, transport by sea is well established for both domestic and international trade. Although the growth of the road network has led to the ending of most shipping along the mainland coast, communication with the rest of Europe and with the 1,500 islands (of which 150 are inhabited) has seen the development and continued growth of a network whose complexity and constantly changing nature can be baffling but is always intriguing.

Europe's first advanced civilisation, the Minoans, occupied Crete and the Aegean islands two thousand years before the birth of Christ. There was never a unified Greek state in ancient times but a union of Greek cities existed well before the foundation of the Olympic Games in 776BC and by 480BC it was possible for the Greek armies and navies to unite and thus defeat the Persians at the battles of Marathon and Salamis and establish Greek supremacy in the eastern Mediterranean. The resulting prosperity marked the high point of democracy in Athens, a concept that originated in Greece and has spread around the world. Economic success provided an environment in which the arts flourished and which produced some of the most sublime works of architecture the world has seen.

From that peak of civilisation, Greece degenerated into war between the various city-states which steadily came under Roman rule from 200BC. The country did not re-emerge as an independent and recognisable nation until finally wresting her freedom from Turkey in 1832, while the northern parts of the country remained as Turkish provinces until as recently as 1912. Even as this book was being prepared for publication, continued strains in Greece's relationship with her neighbours to the north which have emerged from the collapse of the former Yugoslavia and also in the Aegean Sea with Turkey have

Below: *An aerial view of the El Venizelos leaving Igoumenitsa for Trieste.*

Above: *The Flying Dolphin X at speed off Hydra.*

inspired fresh constraints on international trade. These factors have helped Greece to develop an idiosyncratic and independent approach up to the present day. The result is that little trade or transport takes place across Greece's northern land borders and relatively little sea traffic takes place to the east (other than to the independent but culturally connected island of Cyprus). International traffic is therefore focused on the sea routes of the Adriatic and internal communication with the islands is almost entirely achieved by ferry.

Separated from Western Europe during the post-war communist era by her long borders with Albania, Yugoslavia and Bulgaria, Greece continued a largely isolated existence until the 1960s when widespread holiday development and the resulting influx of tourists brought massive change to the country, particularly to the small and previously tranquil islands. With the latitude of parts of the country lying south of the north African coast and surrounded by the warm and beautiful (if occasionally tempestuous) seas of the eastern Mediterranean, Greece woke into the later part of the twentieth century with a start which was to witness an explosion in the ferry services around her shores.

Growing integration with Europe and the collapse of communism in the former Soviet bloc in the eighties briefly led to an increase in road traffic through what was then Yugoslavia. The dismemberment of that unhappy country in the series of wars which have continued through most of the nineties, and the resulting impossibility of regular traffic by road have seen further expansion in the ferry services across the Adriatic. At the same time as the new road and sea connections have opened up Europe to Greek produce, trade has flourished. The fish caught in the waters of Aegean islands can now be loaded onto a lorry and taken by ferry to Athens and on again by sea across the Adriatic to the markets of northern Europe, while the development of cheap air travel which first brought mass tourism to Greece in the 1960s has now opened up other destinations on the far side of the world to inexpensive travel and in turn is now leading to a reduction in the numbers of holiday makers arriving in the country. As the demand for inexpensive travel for budget travellers has tended to decline, the availability of cheap capital and a growing enthusiasm for the passenger shipping business has led to the rapid replacement of older tonnage with a plethora of new construction on the international routes.

Throughout her long history Greece has lived on and around the sea. While much about the ferry system appears at first sight to be peculiar, sometimes even incomprehensible, in reality it represents a logical and highly developed response to history and geography. Greece is not always an easy country for the foreigner to understand, sometimes appearing to be deliberately designed to baffle the stranger. This book aims to introduce the way in which the ferry system operates and the ships which can be found sailing in the warm seas of Greece.

The Ferry System

*T*he subjects of this book cover a wide range of shipping, from motorised caiques of which the wooden hull design can be traced back to ancient times carrying a few passengers from sparsely inhabited islands to nearby villages on the one hand to 30,000 ton ro-pax ferries newly built to the very latest design standards carrying 1,500 passengers and a line of vehicles which extend several kilometres when parked on the quayside. Within this range there is much that is strange to the visitor.

The words 'chaos' and 'politics' both originated in Greece to reflect local conditions and it is wrong to expect the logic and simplicity of northern European practice. There is a wonderful divergence between official control and the most free enterprise imaginable in Greek passenger and freight shipping. Whilst engaging in cut-throat competition, many ferry operators will slavishly follow the same approach as their rivals. An island may have six daily sailings from Athens, yet all may well leave Piraeus within a single hour. The government regulates most elements of the domestic ferry market, even to the price of the coffee in the different classes of cafes aboard ship, yet there are scarcely two weeks in the year when the same pattern of sailings will apply on some routes. It is significant that the post of Shipping Minister is always an important Cabinet post in Greek governments and the current incumbent Stavros Soumakis is adept in the use of the ministry's regulatory powers. The formerly extensive use of subsidies has largely ended, in contrast to the continuing practice elsewhere in Europe, with socially necessary services being provided as a condition of licences for the more lucrative routes.

The European Union has extended until 31st December 2003 the cabotage system which reserves to ships registered in Greece the right to carry passengers between ports within the country, five years after the ending of the system in the rest of Europe. Thus many of the companies sailing on the Adriatic routes will run between the Greek ports of Patras, Igoumenitsa and Corfu before continuing to an Italian port. All will follow a similar itinerary and pick up business at each port, yet those registered under the flags of Cyprus, Italy, Malta or more exotic nations will be unable to carry passengers or freight from a Greek port to a domestic destination, leaving a lucrative short distance trade to Greek owned and crewed ships. Although now the subject of much anxiety amongst Greek ship owners, even in 2004 the right to carry domestic passengers will only be available to ships flagged in other EU countries and even they will still require an operating licence from the Shipping Ministry, a commodity which is hardly ever granted simply or without some political interference.

Operating licences (which are issued to a particular vessel authorising its operations on a specified route) are strictly limited on grounds which too often seem to protect vested interests or to suit political expediency rather than to encourage free enterprise. Superfast Ferries, one of the most innovative of Greek shipping companies who have made an enormous impact on the Adriatic since beginning operations in 1995, have been seeking permission since 1997 to start a new service between Athens and Crete in parallel to the four existing operators. All of them are controlled from Crete and are mainly owned by shareholders on this largest of the Greek islands. Repeated pressure at cabinet level and promises of new tonnage in the future from the current licence holders have left the newcomer, controlled from Athens and with its shareholding widely spread on the Athens Stock Exchange, holding nothing more than a series of notifications of delay in its applications.

The recent problems of the Dodecanese company DANE (described in Chapter 17) would have been simply resolved in a less regulated country by a new operator taking on the immensely lucrative basic route from Rhodes to Piraeus. Instead the Shipping Ministry insisted that as a condition of any new licence modern tonnage be found in a market where it is a rare and expensive commodity and at the same time required potential operators to divert sailings around less populous islands to serve local interests at considerable cost to the operator. The result has been the fossilisation of DANE's operations which have continued notwithstanding the company's financial plight, using old ships on their established routes at the time-honoured schedules.

In 1999 the licensing system was under pressure from the expanding ferry groups to open up established routes to their vessels in place of locally run but often older tonnage. The Ministry has responded by insisting on new licences containing a condition that services will be operated by vessels of less than ten years old but has refused the increase in fares that would be required to justify the cost of investment in such ferries. It must however be expected that this requirement will be enforced with the same flexibility as earlier rules that no vessel older than twenty years could enter the Greek passenger ship register and that withdrawal must take place at 35 years. These regulations are customarily bent by deeming a rebuilding as the date from which such limits are calculated – or simply ignored where compliance is impossible.

Equally, the operators on the more lucrative routes in the Cyclades (whose summer sailings are full to the gunwales with foreign tourists and who have a healthy year round trade carrying supplies between the islands and the mainland) will usually be required to divert their ships once or twice each week throughout the year to serve small, isolated and unremunerative ports to provide a subsidy free social service. It is not for outsiders to offer criticism of such a system. It works in its own way at least as well as alternatives in other countries, but does so in a way which is uniquely and uncompromisingly Greek.

However Byzantine the complexity of the licensing system, the requirements to provide services of defined frequency and routing do ensure that almost all islands enjoy a regular service to the mainland throughout the year. In summer the services will increase to a frenzy but even in mid-winter competing services will be found on all but the least remunerative routes. It is a condition of licences that agreed services are maintained on defined frequencies and the delicate balance of regulation and free enterprise largely works. The operation of the eighty plus fast ferries now in operation is rather different with higher fares permitted and no obligation being imposed to operate outside the summer season.

Above: *On passage across the Gulf of Corinth, a typically full load aboard a landing craft headed for Rion. The use of every square inch of the car deck would make the loading officer on a Cross Channel ship proud but this is an every day occurrence on this most efficient ferry service.*

At the close of the Second World War the Greek merchant marine was in a ruinous state after four years of Nazi occupation and massive losses throughout the war whilst sailing in support of the Allies. Natural skills in the shipping business and inspired support from foreign banks have enabled the national fleet to surpass those of most other European countries in recent decades. At the close of the 1990s the Greek ferry fleet, totalling 807,580 tons in 1998, is second only to Japan both in numbers of vessels and total tonnage while the combined Greek fleet continues to offer greater passenger capacity than any other in the world despite a recent haemorrhage of tonnage of other types of vessel from the Greek shipping register to lower cost and lower tax flags.

The growth of mass tourism to Greece and the availability of a plentiful supply of second hand tonnage from around the globe encouraged a transformation of the ferry fleet from small coasting vessels unloading passengers, goods and prodigious quantities of livestock into tiny tenders off isolated ports as recently as the late 1970s into a modern roll-on roll-off system. It can be bewildering when watching the size of lorries being backed through the stern of a Greek ferry to imagine not merely how they all fit into a vessel deemed surplus elsewhere due to a lack of freight capacity, but also how on earth they all fit on to the road system of the destination island.

As government subsidies have reduced to a comparative trickle, the pace of spending on infrastructure projects has also slowed while the malign influences of the local tabloid press and growing regulation from Brussels have caused faster and less welcome changes in the operation of the system.

There is little doubt that these changes will continue in the years ahead and the style of operation at the end of the twentieth century is likely to give way to a system of operating which is concentrated in the hands of fewer companies operating in a more familiar manner but at the cost of much that is fascinating about the current system.

For over a century Greek ferry operators have turned to the shipping companies of the British Isles and northern Europe to buy outdated vessels for use in their services. Although this practice still continues and many vessels with an interesting past can be found noted in this book, more recently Japanese operators have provided better choices for purchases and over forty ships now in service in Greece began life there. Greek shipyards have tended since the Second World War to specialise in conversion of passenger ships rather than new construction and almost all of the ships described here have been extensively rebuilt for their current operators. The second half of the 1990s has seen a previously unimagined spate of ordering of new ships from shipyards in both northern Europe and the Far East (and even the first orders in twenty years to Greek shipyards) for vessels at a combined cost of over a billion US dollars.

Traditionally a local and often a family business, the ferry industry has been transformed by turning to the Athens Stock Exchange for finance and the capacity to expand. As a result six of the seven largest Greek ferry businesses are now listed on the stock market. It remains to be seen whether the new investors will have the sophistication to take a long-term view of the complexities and fluctuations of this unique part of the shipping industry.

The Ferry Ships

Since the Trojan Wars in the thirteenth century BC, and no doubt for long before, the Greeks have brought their ships into harbour with the stern to the quay. In Book I of the Iliad, Homer describes the oarsmen of the Athenian triremes (galleys with the oars arranged in three layers above one another) reversing their vessels into mooring places where they dropped anchor stones from the bows and made the sterns fast to the shore. This 'Mediterranean Moor' has persisted throughout more than three thousand years and remains universal. As a result, the equally universal habit of painting the ship's name on the stern in Greek letters poses a challenge to modern travellers that will make a little advanced study of the Greek alphabet worthwhile, particularly when seeking a ferry amongst a dozen similar vessels at Patras or Piraeus.

Passengers may find a separate stern gangway, but more usually will have to use the main ramp and dodge the vehicles entering the car deck before finding their own entrance inside. In a few ships, particularly the increasing number which began life in Japan, access to the upper decks from below will be by escalator. Most however, including those of the better lines in the Adriatic, expect the passenger to climb three or four flights of metal staircases with heavy luggage in hand before encountering the reception area. There a rigorous ticket inspection (and on international routes a cursory passport check) can be expected and the process of boarding will be enlivened by the ejection of those who have omitted to board the right ship or bring the right ticket. At times like these the silence of the Greek countryside can seem very distant!

Ships may offer deluxe, first, second, tourist and deck classes, not all ships provide all classes but all can be encountered on the ships plying longer routes. The classes are rigidly separated on board, often with high locked gates. The difference in comfort is impressive on the better ships. First (sometimes styled as 'distinguished' class) and second class will invariably include within the basic fare a berth in a cabin, the former with private facilities; although berths are often not offered on daylight sailings they will always be provided on request. Tourist class will provide a seat in a lounge while deck class means what it says, the passenger will find some internal space of a sort but should be prepared to expect to travel outdoors on the deck. It can be excruciatingly hot on deck on a July day; equally it can be decidedly chilly in the same place at night even in high summer. Restaurants and other facilities on board are comparable with the standards found a decade ago in northern Europe, but with an unmistakable Greek style everywhere. The catering offered and the prices charged will progressively reduce as the class of travel chosen changes.

The crews will invariably be working hours that seem

Below: *The much-rebuilt* **Maria G** *of Med Link Lines seen berthed at Brindisi in 1999 was originally the Japanese ro-ro* **Okudogo 3**. *Her upper vehicle deck provides plenty of ventilation for camping on board with limited cabin accommodation above.*

Above: *A litle advanced study of the Greek alphabet is helpful in identifying your ship. This is the **High Speed I**.*

improbable in Europe in the late 1990s, many working twelve or more hours per day without a day off between Easter and October. On Greek registered vessels the crew will be entirely found from Greek nationals, those sailing under flags of convenience will naturally be more mixed but the staff serving the passengers will still have a very large proportion of Greeks among them. The look of longing on the faces of crew members as they pass their home islands for the umpteenth time in a season with no prospect of visiting their families is one of the more depressing sights aboard otherwise very happy ferry ships. However by the standards of international shipping, crew costs remain high. Not only are historic agreements with trades unions responsible for manning levels now seen as excessive, hotel side crew are still paid on the same scales as other seafarers unlike the norm elsewhere. Simmering discontent at repeated attempts to control crew costs leads to regular action by the Greek Federation of Labour – usually in the form of short strikes on Aegean ferries in August.

On the international services there will be more facilities than on domestic routes and because the fares are not regulated by the government there can be a margin to support greater luxury which helps to separate the competing companies in the Adriatic. This may include swimming pools with water in (rather than a net over the top), casinos and very small shops previously used for limited duty free sales. On domestic services, even the long ones, facilities are unlikely to extend beyond restaurants and lounges – strict control of fares by the

government means that there is little incentive to provide expensive facilities for travellers and little difference in the standards offered between competing companies. However, all vessels will have catering facilities, even landing craft ferries will have a small coffee shop aboard, and on domestic routes the prices in the bars and restaurants will be the subject of government control.

Whatever the idiosyncrasies of the operation, there will be the light and tang of the Mediterranean with a sense of purpose no cruise ship can ever offer.

On shorter crossings, where the occasionally tempestuous waters around the coast of Greece can be expected to cause less distress, the design of the standard vessel is derived from Second World War landing craft. There are currently more than sixty of these vessels in

service, they invariably load only over the bow and will usually be operated by consortia of local operators. On the longer of these routes such as that between Igoumenitsa and Corfu a regular timetable will operate, while on shorter routes such as the twenty minute crossing of the mouth of the Gulf of Corinth at Rion twenty or more ferry ships operate without any timetable, several filling simultaneously at each port and sailing as soon as they are full. Greek motorists seem particularly adept at parking on vessels of this sort and the full capacity can be expected to be exploited by the crew, many of who will be part owners of the vessels and eager to squeeze a little extra profit out of each crossing. However, amongst the apparent anarchy of the arrangements, a consortium will provide underlying stability with vessels departing according to a predetermined order, coming on and off service at prescribed times and sharing the limited load available in the slack seasons. With the exception of the Corfu service in which the Agapitos companies both participate, these routes are of little interest to the major operators and are usually in the hands of local businesses. While often unsophisticated, they provide a simple and regular service which can stand comparison with similar crossings in most other European countries.

One of the less expected features of ferry services between the islands and the mainland (although less common in the Aegean) is the number of long distance buses that are carried on many crossings. The same mixture of independence and regulation that marks the ferry services has also led to long distance buses in each county being collected into a Joint Pool of Bus Owners, the initials of which (in Greek) are KTEL. The larger islands are usually also counties and so control their own KTELs and, since regulation strictly prohibits a bus originating in one county from picking up passengers in another, the only

way in which (for example) a bus from Corfu county can carry passengers on the mainland is to have brought them with it from the island – so the passengers will board at the island bus station and be driven two hundred yards to the ferry port, the bus will be shipped for one and a half hours to the mainland where the passengers will rejoin it and the bus will then continue to Athens. It will be able to drop off passengers at any point en route, but not pick any up since they have to catch a bus which has begun its journey in the county in which they wish to join it. On the return journey the bus can pick up passengers anywhere but only to set down within the destination county. This leads to considerable traffic on the ferries and the sight of milling bus passengers on the quayside as vessels load and unload contributes to the ways in which Greek ferry operation differs so much from the wider European standard.

A study of the Fleet List in Part 5 of this book will show that 75% of the ships in operation in 1999 had exceeded twenty years of age and nearly 25% had passed thirty years. A massive process of renewal will be needed in the coming years to meet the twin challenges of tightening safety regulations and the end of cabotage.

The idiosyncrasy of Greek ferry operation occasionally produces excited and ill-informed criticism in the European press and consumer associations. There is little doubt that the enforcement of bureaucratic regulations is not a priority in many areas of Greek life leaving much for visitors from less happy lands to criticise but the safety record of the ferry industry in the last thirty years compares favourably with that of northern Europe.

Below: *Neatly berthed besides one another with the aid only of their anchors and stern mooring ropes, LANE Lines'* **Vitsentzos Kornaros***, ANEK's* **Candia** *and Minoan Lines* **Knossos** *await their departure from Piraeus.*

The Ferry Ports

*E*ach port is controlled by a semi-autonomous port authority whose main visible contribution to the traveller is the provision of the only (fairly) reliable source of information about ferry movements during the coming day. Lists of their telephone numbers are published in Greek Travel Pages (see Bibliography) and in local newspapers. A call will usually eventually be connected to someone with a least a smattering of English and often save much time shuttling between the competing offices of the rival companies to find the most convenient departure. Many will also publish a sailing list for the day ahead on the door of the port office, although a basic understanding of at least the Greek alphabet will usually be needed.

In Greece (as in the UK) there is no readily available national source of information about ferry services, but each company operating in a port will have at least one, and usually several competing agencies selling its tickets. These agencies (in Greek – praktoreions) will hardly ever offer tickets or information about all of the ferry lines operating from that port. A traveller should not expect that the praktoreion of one company will divulge information about the existence, let alone the departure times, of its rivals. Prior knowledge of the style of ships that are available, their relative speeds and the standard of accommodation aboard will invariably be available to local travellers but can be extremely difficult for a visitor to obtain, although the increasing use of photographs to advertise the ships will help the observant traveller find the desired style of ship. There is no substitute for making enquiries at all of the competing offices before a booking is made since some services, especially those to the more distant islands of the Cyclades and Dodecanese, make many more stops and take much longer than others. For example the praktoreion of GA Ferries in Rhodes will cheerfully sell travellers tickets to Piraeus on the *Romilda* (originally the *Free Enterprise VIII*) at the same fare as the praktoreion for DANE Lines next door will be selling tickets to the same destination aboard the *Patmos*. Both will sail within an hour of one another, but the former will take a circuitous route via Crete making eight calls in 36 hours while the latter makes a non-stop run to the capital in twelve.

A slightly less frenetic place to do business, but no less partial in the provision of advice, is the Kentriko Grapheion (Central Booking Office) which each company will have in almost every port. They may have no more information about alternatives to offer, but are often much better able to assist with berth allocation and vehicle space reservation.

Until recently each praktoreion would cheerfully sell as many tickets as customers presented themselves seeking them, leaving it to the crew of the ferry to sort out berthing the passengers when they were aboard and to maintain at least a pretence of preventing overloading. However, a few well publicised incidents of gross overcrowding (e.g. the *Express Olympia* ex-*Earl Granville* with a capacity of 1,500 passengers was found to have over 2,200 aboard when the port police took a surprise, indeed probably unprecedented, interest in the matter one day in 1995) led to a campaign in the tabloid press at the same time as a new Minister of Shipping was appointed. A few unfortunate ship captains were taken off to jail to encourage the others and the Shipping Minister announced the compulsory introduction within an unrealistically short period of computerised ticketing on all vessels to prevent future overbooking.

The system is now in general but far from universal use but, since most praktoreions lack both the enthusiasm and finance to install the necessary computer terminals for each line they represent, much shouting into telephones is now involved before the same type of multi-part paper ticket is torn from a pad as has been used in past generations. It carries little obvious indication whether or not a computer has blessed it first. Again, the Kentriko Grapheion will often reduce the hassle if not the time of this exercise.

It is worth bearing in mind that intermediate traffic on longer distance routes is permitted, indeed greatly encouraged. The booking systems in use do not necessarily provide assistance with journeys of this sort and clarity about the availability of a berth from an intermediate port is not to be taken for granted.

The passenger, with or without vehicle or ticket, will then find that the process of boarding will verge between the unsupervised and the more exciting with several members of the crew and port police giving loud, simultaneous but conflicting instructions in a dialect of Greek one will often not previously have encountered. Although alien for most visitors from more orderly lands, the boarding and parking of one's vehicle will be achieved with little trauma but by a process that owes more to magic than management.

The linkspan is unknown in Greece. With tides averaging fifteen centimetres in the eastern Mediterranean and careful placing of breakwaters to avoid strong currents, all that is needed at a successful port is a suitable depth of water, a strong cement wall about a metre above water level and a few well placed bollards to attach stern ropes. An arriving ferry will invariably drop one or both of her anchors at each port as she goes astern to the quay to make her 'Mediterranean Moor'. The stern ramp will be lowered almost to quay height, usually at a considerable distance from the berth. Foot passengers usually disembark via the vehicle deck and the very short time in port at intermediate calls, often no more than ten minutes for disembarkation of foot and vehicle traffic and the collection of a substantial onward load, will mean that all will be assembled by the ramp in readiness for arrival, perhaps restrained by a rope, or perhaps not. The ship will go astern straight up to the quay, usually with no hesitation or fuss, and will stop with a metre or so of

F/B ΒΙΤΣΕΝΤΖΟΣ ΚΟΡΝΑΡΟΣ

το πιο φιλόξενο πλοίο του Αιγαίου...

LANE

Πειραιάς - Μήλος - Άγιος Νικόλαος
Σητεία - Κάσος - Κάρπαθος

Above: *The praktoreion of one company will not divulge information about the services of its rivals.*

clear water to be bridged by her stern ramp. Despite the exhausting schedules and fierce competition between operators, the quality of seamanship is not to be doubted.

During this approach two distinct activities will have been taking place ashore. The crowd of potential passengers and hangers about who will have moved up to the water's edge during the half hour before the ship's arrival will be corralled to an area far from where they expect to want to be by the local port police. Whether at a busy port like Patras or a small island port with only a couple ships calling each week, there will be a solid representation of these immaculately turned out officers in all white uniforms with much gold braid. Their exact purpose can be difficult to discern, certainly it does not appear to instil much order into proceedings, but it does give an excellent opportunity for the trait of whistle blowing which appears to play such an important part in the outdoor life of a country where silence is seen as unmasculine.

The other activity that will be taking place will be that a couple of unshaven men will have detached themselves from the crowd and been revealed as the rope men who place hawsers from the stern of the arriving ship onto the bollards and then retire. With the aid of her ropes, her anchors and not least her main engines – but none of the technology on which so much reliance is placed elsewhere – the officers and crew will accomplish a berthing as difficult as bringing a vessel into an English Channel port but with far less fuss. Equally the northern European obsession to separate the passenger from the side of the harbour has no place in a Greek port yet accidents seem to be avoided by the obviousness of the potential danger.

Recently the port authority in Patras has commissioned a study by the Dover Harbour Board into the possibility of modernising the facilities for loading ships, but no change seems likely in the absence of greater demand from the operators and a greater willingness to pay substantial port charges. Although there are now a considerable number of ferries with the capacity for double deck loading in operation on the Adriatic, the minimal cost of the current installation compared to the likely alternative has so far kept demand for changes from even such advanced operators as Superfast Ferries to little more than a public relations gambit.

The use of opening bows on Greek ferries (other than landing craft) has always been virtually non-existent. Most are welded shut, but in a few cases some will be opened to assist in exhaust dispersal when heavy lorries are carried. Other than the landing craft, only the *Polaris* of Ventouris Ferries and the little *Karistos* of Mililis Lines regularly use their bow doors. In the case of the former the reason is the arrangement of her internal ramps while the latter can be explained simply since she lacks a stern door!

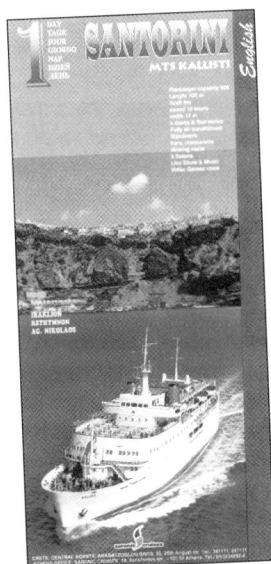

Part 2 - The Adriatic
Ferry Services on Western Greece

The whole length of the Adriatic Sea from Trieste at the north, on the borders of Italy and the modern Slovenia, to Cape Matapan at the southernmost point of the Greek mainland sees regular Greek ferry services. They vary in style between the long-haul routes from northern destinations such as Venice and Trieste to Turkey on crossings of two or three days and on the other hand five-minute passages of landing craft in sheltered waters. However, apart from a few operations between Italy and Turkey not calling at Greek ports, there are at present no passenger services through the Corinth Canal and very few passing around the south coast of the Peloponnese linking the Western with the Eastern sides of Greece. The style of operation in the Adriatic is in many cases very different from that encountered in the Aegean, described in Part 3.

Historically the first regular ferry services across the Adriatic were those established by the Romans linking Brindisi on the heel of Italy, at the end of the Via Appia from Rome, with Durres in modern Albania at the start of the Via Egnatia crossing Greece and Thrace to reach Constantinople (modern Istanbul) and the eastern Roman Empire beyond. Although regular steamers have crossed from Venice, Ancona and Brindisi to the Greek ports since the nineteenth century, the character of the services has changed radically in the course of the last twenty-five years.

In the mid-nineteen seventies the services were principally provided by the state-owned Greek and Italian shipping lines, Hellenic Mediterranean Lines and Adriatica. Although both commissioned car ferries on the route from Brindisi in 1960, the longer distance routes were seen as conventional liner services until the early 1980s. Chandris and later Karageorgis Lines used converted ocean ships, including one former Union-Castle liner, unusually equipped for side loading of vehicles, until the 1990s. They carried mainly passengers and their baggage, whilst freight was either transported in bulk by sea or alternatively subjected to the long and hot railway passage through the communist controlled countries of the Balkans.

The growth of mass tourism in Greece and the increasing availability of second-hand car ferries from northern Europe and then Japan during the 1970s encouraged the proliferation of passenger services from Ancona, Bari and above all from Brindisi but many operated purely on a seasonal basis. The great changes that membership of the European Union has given Greece are mentioned elsewhere but their greatest impact on the ferry services has been in the growth of lorry traffic, developing simultaneously with the massive improvement of the Greek road system. These have led to the establishment of regular freight services, first from Piraeus and Corinth and later from the western ports of Patras and Igoumenitsa to Italy.

The collapse of the communist government in Yugoslavia and the subsequent disintegration of that country has prevented traffic from making any very extensive use of the road network in the Balkans and driven many visitors from the area. At the same time the massive development of the Italian network of autostrada and the more limited construction of motorways in Greece have made possible the development of the network of ferry services either devoted exclusively to the needs of freight traffic or carrying large quantities of massive lorries alongside tourist vehicles.

Initially, the demand for ferry ships was provided almost entirely by second-hand tonnage, Greek ship owners having been particularly effective at spotting suitable vessels from all corners of the globe and rebuilding them to suit the potential traffic. However, two landmarks in the

Below: *The Port Police prepare for action. An important discussion takes place as Agoudimos Line's Kapetan Alexandros A arrives.*

Left: *Deck class travel. A game of backgammon helps to pass the time for the passengers who have not booked accommodation.*

European Union travels mainly via Patras to Ancona and Venice while transit traffic from Turkey is carried in great quantity via Igoumenitsa. The latter, including regular heavy lorries from Iran and the new republics which have emerged from the southern part of the former Soviet Union, mainly require cheap passages regardless of the speed of the ship and mostly sail to Bari or Brindisi. Similarly passenger traffic to Greece is aimed mainly through Patras (with holiday business to Corfu and the Ionian islands) while there is an enormous market for Turkish gastarbeiters (migrant workers) returning home from Germany and elsewhere in northern Europe. Despite driving expensive cars such as Mercedes they seek out the cheapest possible passages and will make use of the bargain operators which constantly emerge and disappear in this sector while avoiding the better specified but more expensive operators on the long-haul routes.

current services are the introduction of a regular Minoan Lines service from Patras in 1981 using the Japanese-built *El Greco* (a ship still in service but now in the Aegean) and the introduction of the revolutionary services of Superfast Ferries in 1995 and their subsequent development. Each in turn has introduced a new vibrancy into both the passenger market and the freight business which provides year round profitability. The two companies have emerged as the principal players in what still remains a highly competitive market offering a proliferation of different services which together provide an unrivalled variety of vessels serving the Greek Adriatic ports.

Today the freight and passenger services contain diverse elements. Extensive freight from Greece to the

Domestic services in the Adriatic are concentrated on the Ionian Islands. They vary between Corfu, only five kilometres off the Albanian coast, with its regular ferry service provided mainly by landing craft ferries on the ninety minute passage from Igoumenitsa, to the longer distance services occupying passages of up to four and a half hours to the more distant islands of Kefalonia and Ithaca and served particularly by the blue ships of Strintzis Lines.

The short passages at Preveza and Rion are entirely provided by landing craft type ferries and offer a style and efficiency of service which is rarely matched elsewhere.

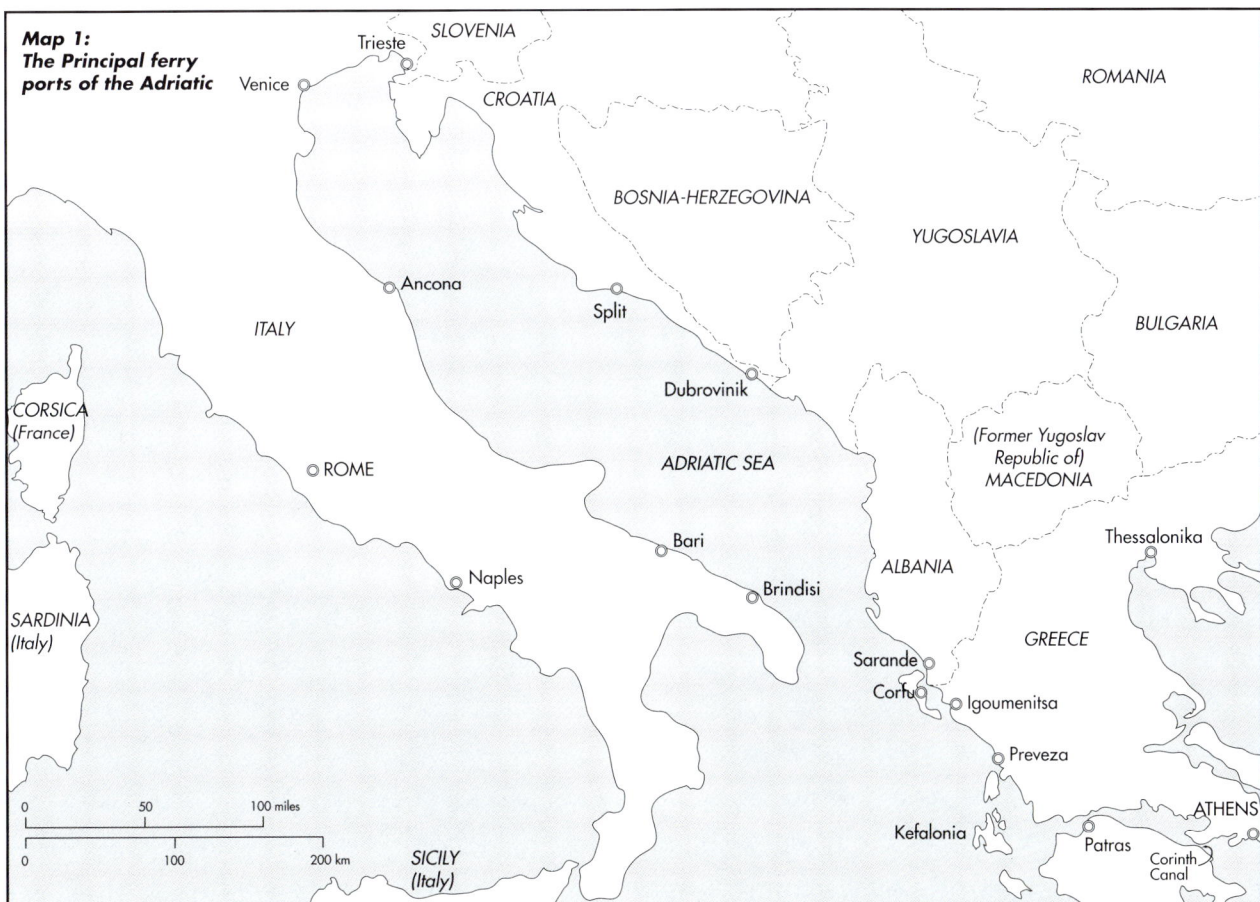

Map 1:
The Principal ferry ports of the Adriatic

Chapter 6

Long-Haul International Services

Venice

Historically the more distant services have come to Greece from Venice, at the north-western corner of the Adriatic. Still an important port for departure of both Minoan and Strintzis Lines as well as an assortment of freight operators to Turkey (outside the scope of this book) Venice none the less plays a comparatively minor part in ferry schedules. The number of truly long-haul services operating in the Adriatic is surprisingly small, but reflects the easy availability of cheap air fares for passenger traffic and the excellent motorway networks in Italy and Greece for freight traffic which make long sea passages comparatively uneconomic. Passengers lucky enough to depart from this most beautiful of Mediterranean cities will sail from the Stazione Maritimma beside the railway station at the end of the causeway carrying wheeled traffic into the city of canals. The journey to the open sea, past the Grand Canal and St. Mark's Basilica, gives some of the most memorable sights to be enjoyed from the deck of a European ferry. Mistress of the Adriatic for four centuries and more, Venice remains the titular headquarters of Adriatica Lines, but is not currently served by them. Their wonderful cruise ferry service from Venice via Corfu and Patras to Port Said in Egypt has fallen victim to the political turmoil in the Middle East and the furthest that the ordinary passenger can currently venture is to Patras, a distance of 608 nautical miles. During 1995 and 1996 Minoan and Strintzis combined their operations and gave a daily service, but the dissolution of that alliance in 1997 led to a cutback in services which was made good in 1998 by the delivery of new tonnage to both companies. In 1999 Minoan offered daily departures in summer (five times weekly throughout the winter) and Strintzis sailed four times weekly (twice in winter). The current passage time of 36 hours to Patras will be much reduced with the introduction of the two new ships currently under construction in South Korea for Minoan which advertise journeys of no more than 21 hours.

Trieste

The idiosyncratic port of Trieste, at the very division between western and eastern Europe but fitting comfortably into neither, has for some years been served only by ANEK Lines of Crete, who have operated five times weekly in summer and twice in winter on the longest route in the Adriatic – a distance of 625 nautical miles. However, the mounting pressure of competition seems likely to lead to a reduction in frequency of the service and in 1999 two of the weekly sailings have not run further south than Igoumenitsa.

Ancona

Ancona, due east of Florence and well situated on the Italian autostrada network to receive traffic from all parts of western Europe, is 504 nautical miles from Patras. For long seen as a 36-hour crossing, including stops at Corfu and Igoumenitsa, recent developments in higher speed operation of ferries have brought this unattractive shipbuilding town within nineteen hours of Patras by the non-stop services of Superfast Ferries, making possible daily sailings between the ports with the pair of vessels delivered in 1998 to this enterprising company. Minoan Lines also operate their flagship service between Ancona and Patras, using a pair of ships also delivered in 1998 built at the Fosen yard in Norway. Potentially the equals of the Superfast ships they are forced to fit a call at Igoumenitsa into their sailings which are thus extended to a twenty-hour schedule which is often exceeded due to delays at the intermediate port. Although the company is confident that the extra traffic carried to northern Greece fully compensates for the loss of a round trip each week, the inability to provide a departure

Below: *The funnel of* **Superfast IV**.

Above: *One of a pair of genuinely high-speed ships built for Minoan in 1998, the **Ikarus** catches the evening sun as she turns onto her berth at Patras on arrival from Ancona.*

on a uniform daily basis must give considerable help to Superfast in the express market at the expense of the Cretan company. Being within a (long) day's road journey from much of France and Germany, Ancona represents an ideal compromise between road and sea travel for much traffic to and from Greece. A further growth in services through the port is likely as more new vessels are delivered to Superfast who are likely to introduce a second daily service in each direction.

In addition to several services to the long coast of Croatia, Ancona also receives an almost daily service by ANEK operating two unattractive former Japanese ferries to Patras on a 24-hour schedule which they do not always manage. Some sailings make long intermediate calls at Igoumenitsa. Strintzis Lines have long provided a comfortable if slower service with their own pair of former Japanese ferries, but entered the 23-hour market in 1999 with newly reconditioned former Japanese tonnage. Although both companies have new ships on order, at present they threaten to provide too little comfort at a speed which is not quite fast enough to attract much of the passenger traffic on offer, but do at least offer the prospect of an intensive fares war on the route.

The massive investment by rival companies has left Marlines, who have operated an interesting fleet of former northern European vessels from Ancona to Corfu, Igoumenitsa and Patras since 1982 struggling to answer the competition. In 1999 their efforts were concentrated on

Above: *One of Strintzis' two ex-Japanese ferries of 1972 which have given long service on the Adriatic routes, the **Ionian Galaxy** seen as speed.*

Above: *Late evening in Patras as Strintzis' **Ionian Star** (since sold) arrives in front of the **Aretousa** while **Superfast I** loads on her berth.*

operations from Bari and serious opposition from them is now unlikely on the longer route. Their former operation with the *Charm M* between Ancona, Patras, Heraklion in Crete and Kusadasi in Turkey also failed to operate since 1998 and the disposal of this ship to operate in the Black Sea has left a gap in the operations on this interesting route.

Turkish Routes

The long distance freight vessels running from northern Italian ports to Turkey and the Middle East sometimes make unannounced calls at Greek ports but lie outside the scope of this book.

Croatia

The other long-haul ferry route is of a very different sort. It is that provided by the Yugoslavian (now Croatian) company Jadrolinija operating a complicated weekly timetable along the whole length of the Croatian coast from Rijeka via Split and Dubrovnik (and a number of other intermediate ports) to Igoumenitsa. The 36-hour passage is one of the loveliest in the Adriatic, passing close to the beautiful shoreline and between the islands of Croatia and the Dalmatian coast and then following the wild and empty mountain coast of Albania, sometimes diverting via Bari on the way.

Below: *The most stunning background for a ferry, Minoan Lines **Daedalus** passing the Doge's Palace and the campanile of St.Mark's Basilica in Venice on arrival from Patras in 1998.*

Shorter International Routes

Chapter 7

Bari

The Italian port of Bari, due east of Naples and effectively at the end of the Italian autostrada along the east coast of the country, has throughout the 1980s and 90s enjoyed a prolific ferry business with Greece. The introduction of much faster tonnage from Ancona, three hundred kilometres north and nearer to the main population centres of northern Europe, has seen a spectacular decline in number of ships serving the port from Greece in recent times. It is, however at a distance which makes a non-stop passage to Patras in less than twenty-four hours entirely practicable even with relatively elderly tonnage. Bari also sees a considerable trade to the ports of Albania and the countries of the former Yugoslav republic.

Pride of place among the current operators from Bari once again belongs to Superfast Ferries who moved their excellent initial pair of vessels to sail from here after the second pair took their place on the main Ancona route. Comparable to the best modern ferries elsewhere in Europe they have badly damaged the trade of the other companies operating older if more interesting tonnage with their daily sixteen-hour sailings to Patras via Igoumenitsa.

Bari has long been the principal Italian port served by Ventouris Ferries who, until 1998 operated five ships to the port. The subsequent disposal of the cavernous *Polaris* to Scandinavia and the charter of her sister *Venus* to St Malo-Cork Ferries (contingencies which would have seemed implausible until very recently) and the lack of new investment in this surviving part of the Ventouris empire has cast doubt on the service for the future. While there is a clearly established market, it shows signs of being undermined by the competition on the longer routes and an onset of predatory pricing on the services to Brindisi.

Poseidon Lines are operators at the less expensive end of the Adriatic ferry business, using their ex-Japanese ships on changing routes to exploit possibilities as they develop. Having concentrated on the eastern Mediterranean for some years, and not operating to Italy at all in 1998, they returned to run between Bari and Igoumenitsa in 1999 on a daily thirteen-hour crossing.

The other company operating regularly to Greece from Bari in 1999 was Marlines, who provide an interesting pair of ships (the *Duchess M*, previously the former Brittany Ferries vessel *Breizh-Izel*, and the *Countess M*, previously P&O's *Leopard*) operating to Igoumenitsa. Their facilities and twelve-hour crossing times stand up well to the competition on that route provided by Ventouris, but not to close scrutiny with the other Adriatic routes and the constant adjustment of the timetables by Marlines suggests that a further change in their services is to be expected.

An unexpected return to Adriatic trade was made in 1999 by A.K. Ventouris operating the mainly freight-carrying *Euromagique* to Patras three times per week on an eighteen-hour schedule. In recent years Arkadia Lines have operated to Bari, but has not served the port since 1997. With the exception of the Superfast Ferries service a further decline in the importance of the port as a link to Greece seems inevitable.

Brindisi

The services from the port of Brindisi are of a different character from those operating into the northern Adriatic both

Below: *Contrasting vessels in the port of Bari – Ventouris Ferries'* **Athens Express**, *the* **Superfast II** *and Stern Lines' laid-up* **Çesme Stern** *– originally Thoresen's* **Viking II**.

Above: *The **Superfast II**, seen loading for Bari at Patras with the 2000-metre high mountains of Achaia behind, demonstrating the immaculate presentation of her operators.*

in the age and style of ships that operate on them and the traffic that they carry. From Brindisi it is only two hundred kilometres to the mainland port of Igoumenitsa and this presents the opportunity of a round trip in twenty four hours even to ships which have long since celebrated their thirtieth birthday. Passengers do not often choose to travel from Brindisi because of the pleasures of life in south-eastern Italy, it is a long and slow journey beyond the reach of the autostrada and express trains; they come this way because it is the shortest and cheapest route. While the wealthier tourists and the refrigerated lorries collecting loads of perishable fruit and vegetables from Greek markets for consumption in northern Europe will head to Ancona and the northern ports, the passenger decks of the ferries from Brindisi will carry a good mixture of students on Inter-Rail passes and other passengers travelling at the cheapest possible fares. A significant number will be Turkish 'gastarbeiters' in improbably expensive vehicles travelling with their large families between their temporary work in Germany and their homes in Anatolia. Much of the freight will also be destined for the long drive across northern Greece to Turkey and onto the Middle East. This sector of the market demands above all else inexpensive fares and looks for little in the way of sophistication in the accommodation provided.

If the traveller is unlikely to choose the routes from Brindisi for the sophistication of his travelling companions, he will at least be rewarded by the complex network of services provided by a dozen shipping lines using ships of all ages and types and flying the flags of countries from lands well beyond the eastern Mediterranean. While some continue to Patras, an increasing segment of the ships in this market carry long distance passengers and freight to Igoumenitsa as an interruption in the long drive to Turkey while a decreasing part of the market consists of holiday makers travelling to Corfu.

The Sea Containers group has expressed a strong interest in acquiring a share of the business heading for Turkey both by announcing an intention to bid for control of Turkish Mediterranean Lines when the business is privatised and by introducing a high-speed passenger service. The concept of a fifteen-hour passage in a fast craft is not an immediately attractive one and would also appear to pose considerable logistical difficulties if it is ever to come into operation.

A further indication of coming change is the announcement by Strintzis Lines of their intention to place one of the large vessels now being built in the Netherlands onto a Brindisi to Patras service in 2000. If their gamble succeeds it will inevitably lead to a major change in the current operations from the port.

Otranto

Further to the south of Brindisi, at the very stiletto of Italy's heel, is the small port of Otranto. Although offering the shortest of all sea crossings, it is too far off the road and rail network to offer much traffic and recently all ferry operators, including latterly even Hellenic Mediterranean Lines, have withdrawn in favour of Brindisi.

Albania

Throughout history Albania has been a wild if stunningly beautiful area of mountains and eagles but since the departure of the Turks in 1912 it has enjoyed little peace or prosperity. The extraordinary isolation produced by the fanatical socialist government of Enver Hoxha saw this impoverished country entirely isolated from its neighbours. The first sporadic ferry services from Corfu, separated from Albania by a channel only three kilometres wide, did not start operations until 1990. The passenger service continues to operate four days per week between the southern Albanian port of Sarande and Corfu using former Royal Navy Ham class inshore minesweepers suitably converted for the task. The unsettling welcome the traveller receives in Sarande, one of the principal transit points for drug traffic into western Europe, contrasts favourably with the extreme suspicion that the Albanian traveller receives from the Greek immigration authorities in Corfu. Their anxiety extends beyond the detection of narcotics to the even more pressing desire of most Greeks to exclude economic migrants from Albania prepared to undertake manual labour at wages well below those acceptable to an increasingly sophisticated and western focused Greek population.

Reports of western aid to Albania from time to time suggest the establishment of regular vehicle ferry services from Patras to Albanian ports, but these have never achieved any regularity. In 1998 a twice weekly service using a landing craft ferry between Sarande and Igoumenitsa was inaugurated but it attracted little traffic, due no doubt to the appalling state of the roads inland from Sarande over some of Europe's emptiest and most precipitous mountains. Since 1998 Vefa Lines have operated the much-travelled *Aulona* on a route from Durres, the main port of Albania, to Patras, mainly to transport international aid. However neither service has appeared to prosper.

Domestic Services

*T*he Eptanisa, or Seven Islands, of Greece in the Ionian Sea are among the greenest and most fertile parts of the country and produce considerable agricultural traffic as well as providing some of the best known and most developed tourist destinations in the western part of the country. They provide a diverse mixture of ferry services.

In addition to its role as the first port of call for many of the international ferry services in the Adriatic, Corfu enjoys a frequency of service which, at least until it is examined carefully, appears recognisable in the more regulated areas of northern Europe. The ninety minute passages from Corfu town (towards the north of the island) and from the southern village of Lefkimmi to Igoumenitsa do not, however, enjoy a standard of sophistication which would recognised by passengers on

Above: *The* **Pantokrator** *berthing in Corfu in the evening, unrecognisable as a 'Superflex' class double-ended vessel from which she was converted.*

Bottom Right: *The Newhaven/Dieppe car ferry the* **Villandry** *served in Strintzis fleet and is seen as the* **Delos** *at Kilini in 1990. She has recently been sold to India for scrap.*

the Dover to Calais route with sailings of similar duration. With two exceptions the services are provided entirely by landing craft ferries propelled by ancient and all too apparently unsilenced diesel engines offering compact passenger accommodation at the stern, containing nothing more sophisticated than a lounge with over-amplified television and a cafeteria offering toast and coffee. The views of the mountains of Greece and Albania from the open deck are, however, particularly fine.

The landing craft on these routes are provided by a consortium containing both local operators and representatives of both branches of the Agapitos companies and the hourly service is provided through a complicated roster which ensures that all vessels take an equal share both with the busy and lucrative morning and evening sailings and with the virtually empty midday and night sailings. The crews of half a dozen or so will work long spells interrupted by gaps of three to four hours rest while laying over in port awaiting their next turn on the route. Co-operation in the timetable does not extend to matters such as the operation of the booking offices where separate windows will be opened, at hours suitable to the sailings allocated on any particular day, by each

member of the syndicate.

Some relief to and competition with the landing craft is provide by Kerkyra Lines operating a chunky former Japanese ferry and Feax Express Lines operating an admirable conversion of a double ended 'Superflex' class vessel which has emerged as the sleek and single ended *Pantokrator* offering the coldest air conditioning and the most extensive accommodation (but equally limited catering) of all the ships on domestic sailings serving this large and lovely island. These two ships, whilst operating for different companies who again maintain separate ticket offices, operate a co-ordinated schedule with six departures in each direction daily being alternated between the two ships. While quicker and, at least in the case of the *Pantokrator*, more comfortable than the landing craft they compete with, the latter continue to take most of the traffic due to their greater frequency and more convenient departure points within the ports that they serve.

For some years Corfu enjoyed a fast ferry service using the Westamarin catamaran *Nearchos* via Paxos and Preveza to the improbable ferry port of Amphilochia. 3½ hours by this small and noisy vessel from Corfu took the passenger forty kilometres inland from Preveza at the innermost reach of the Ambracian Gulf. Despite the discomfort of the journey, Amphilochia is less than 120 kilometres from Andirrion from where the ferry to Rion (see below) gives connection to the motorway to Athens, halving the road journey across northern Greece and saving at least two hours on the overall journey time. However it is not currently operating and a resumption in service cannot be taken for granted. In 2000 Minoan are to introduce a new fast ferry service from Corfu to Patras using the car carrying catamaran *High Speed I* on a daily service via Igoumenitsa which may spell the end of the local passages from Patras on the ships sailing on to Venice.

It is at present possible to travel by almost any of the Greek registered ships running on the international routes between Corfu or Igoumenitsa and Patras – an eight hour passage usually conducted overnight but offering spectacular coastal scenery on daytime sailings. In contrast to the international legs of the services, the fares and cabin supplements on the domestic part of the route are regulated by the government and the comfort of the first class accommodation provides an attractive and economical alternative to an hotel in Corfu. The cabotage system means that the service is only available on ships registered in Greece and so, whilst possible on all of the vessels of Minoan Lines

Left: *The Westamarin catamaran* **Nearchos** *of Cretan Ferries leaving Corfu on her daily run to Amphilochia.*

injection of European Union money. Its opening, which is not yet imminent, will no doubt speed the passage of motor vehicles through north-western Greece which in turn, particularly if the proposed fixed link between Andirrion and Rion is eventually constructed, will no doubt lead to a steady removal of ferry services from Patras to Igoumenitsa.

The Rion ferry service, crossing the mouth of the Gulf of Corinth to Andirrion in twenty minutes, is much the busiest and most frequent of all ferry services in Greece and perhaps all Europe. Operated by a fleet of landing craft providing similar facilities to those serving Corfu, it again provides a complicated co-operative of owners with an opportunity to operate on rosters that a provide a balance of loads and profits throughout the year while maintaining a service at least hourly during the middle of the night and, at the busier times of the day, departing at intervals of as little as two minutes with up to four ships loading simultaneously at each port. Although the increasing size of modern vessels means that few can now travel by ferry through the Corinth Canal into the Aegean, the short crossing provides stunning views of the mountains on both sides of the Gulf and the occasional opportunity to see passing shipping as a welcome break in long road journeys between northern Greece and the terrifying National Highway (motorway) from Patras to Athens.

and ANEK, it can only be managed on about half of the vessels in the Strintzis fleet while none of the other vessels on international service in 1999 qualified. Similar arrangements apply from Igoumenitsa but it should be noted that domestic passengers are not carried on the Minoan Lines Express service to Ancona or the Superfast service to Bari where the speed of the international journey is considered more important that the loss of domestic revenue, an unfortunate omission which the introduction of fast craft is unlikely to remedy.

The island of Paxos sees little serious ferry traffic beyond thrice-weekly visits from Hellenic Mediterranean Lines on their Brindisi service, passenger motorboats from Corfu and a single landing craft carrying vehicles to Igoumenitsa. The catamaran *Nearchos* called here when operating on the route from Corfu to Amphilochia and the daily service of Misano Alta Velocita Lines to Brindisi starts from here, but neither appears to do much business at an island whose main focus is the package holiday.

The southern Ionian islands of Kefalonia and Ithaca enjoy an unchanging service with Strintzis Lines' substantial ferry *Kefalonia* running twice daily from Patras and providing the only regular domestic service from the immensely busy international port. Kefalonia, an elegant island with an interesting history but little architecture from before a massive earthquake in 1953, is also served by the elderly Strintzis ferries *Eptanisos* and *Ionian Sun* from Kilini on the western coast of the Peloponnese, but they will shortly be replaced by a South Korean-built ship. It is however to travel to the unhappily overdeveloped island of Zakynthos that most travellers make their way to the port of Kilini, from where services depart at eight irregular times in the day providing a quality of service that varies between the tolerable and the truly grubby with a variety of locally built vessels. In the early 1990s an alternative route to Zakynthos was provided by a small fleet of Russian-built hydrofoils operating from Patras, but this did not continue after the 1996 season.

The two busiest domestic services in the Adriatic do not, however, serve islands but are short distance car ferry services across narrow channels. The more northerly runs from Preveza across the mouth of the Ambracian Gulf, which is here only one kilometre wide, to the sandy port of Aktion. It was here in 31 BC that the Roman fleet routed the combined navies of Anthony and Cleopatra in the battle of Actium, an event that paved the way for the establishment of the Roman Empire under Augustus. The significance of the location is not, however, matched by the five landing craft that make the ten minute crossing and which are scheduled to be replaced by a tunnel which is to be constructed with the aid of another large

Map 2: The Ionian Islands

ALBANIA

GREECE

Corfu

Corfu

Igoumenitsa

Lefkimmi

Paxos

Preveza

Amfilochia

IONIAN SEA

Lefkas

Andirrion

Rion

Aegion

Patras

Kefalonia

Kilini

Zakynthos

Zakynthos

PELOPONNESE

Kalamata

0   25   50 km

0   25   50 miles

Adriatic Ports

Chapter 9

Patras

Backed by the magnificent 2,000 metre high mountains of Achaia and facing out across the mouth of the Gulf of Corinth towards the equally impressive mountains of Aetolia, Patras serves as Greece's second most important ferry port. Regrettably its beautiful situation and busy harbour sandwich a singularly ugly town with the single redeeming feature of a modern gem of a cathedral in which is venerated the head of St. Andrew the Apostle.

The ferry port occupies approximately one kilometre of the sea front and on busy summer days can contain fifteen ferries loading simultaneously for Italian ports. Most shipping lines have their central booking offices along the road that could be an esplanade were it not a principal part of the one-way system carrying an incessant traffic of lorries, buses and other vehicles from Athens to western Greece as well as the narrow gauge Peloponnesian Railway and a high fence surrounding the port. In the same street can be found a single good hotel and a couple of useful shipping offices as well as many other travel agents, hotels and restaurants of all qualities below good.

The harbour itself is, however, attractive and accessible. The high fence that surrounds it is an ostentatious show of the customs and immigration checks which are casually observed for international traffic but easily by-passed by pedestrians through numerous open gates leading to harbour front cafes.

The pattern of operations has traditionally been for the harbour to be empty of ships during the night, with a half dozen of the faster ferries arriving from Italian ports between seven and nine in the morning which rapidly unload and settle down for a day's slumber at their berths while slower ships arrive progressively during the day until, by five in the evening, all will be beginning to load for departures during the course of the evening. This pattern, like so many others, is not followed by the Superfast ships or those on Minoan Lines express service to Ancona which settle for three to four hour turn round times, but again in the late afternoon. The increasing competition on Adriatic routes is however making long turnarounds in port unacceptable and ANEK even timetable arrivals in the middle of the night to maximise use of their vessels – not necessarily the most pleasant way of arriving in Greece.

As noted in Chapter 4, Patras shares with all other Greek ports an extreme simplicity of infrastructure. Beyond a concrete quay of considerable length and numerous mooring bollards, it amounts to little more than a duty free shop doing good business in 1999, despite the official abolition of such facilities for travel within Europe, and numerous cabins for the port police to rest in between bouts of whistle blowing. Although it was announced at the launch of the Superfast Ferries services to Ancona in 1995 that double deck loading would be provided, nothing has happened and no such development is anticipated in the near future. It is, indeed, unusual for the ships of any particular line to berth in the same location on successive days and while most vessels are equipped for single deck loading only, the introduction of more complicated facilities seems highly unlikely.

Although much holiday traffic heads south from Patras to the wild mountains and beautiful beaches of the Peloponnese, the great majority of the traffic from the ships heads eastward from the port on the National Highway, a dual carriageway supposedly of motorway

Below: *Older vessels at Patras – Med Link Lines' **Afrodite II**, the **Vergina** and HML's **Egnatia** (both since withdrawn) and HML's **Media II**.*

Above: *Adriatica Lines' Egitto Express arriving in Patras from Brindisi with her anchors ready to release.*

standard but in reality full of unexpected hazards which carries more traffic than it can conveniently handle along the south coast of the Gulf of Corinth and on to Athens.

Kilini

Sixty kilometres south west of Patras is the dusty port of Kilini, from where ships sail eight times daily on the one and a half-hour passage to Zakynthos and twice daily on the three hour sailing to Kefalonia. It has recently benefited from a new port building containing pleasant cafes and shops. Kilini lacks the magnificent setting of the other Adriatic ferry ports despite being overlooked by a fine medieval castle. It is a casual and relaxed place with an excellent beach immediately outside the harbour mole. Kilini shares with Piraeus and Patras the possibility of extremely convenient railway connections, the station immediately adjoins the ferry terminal and has had regular rail connections on the narrow gauge line running to Patras and Athens as well as circling the Peloponnese. Regrettably despite large continuing investment in railways elsewhere in Greece, this branch line has not operated since 1997 and an early restoration of services seems improbable. Bus links are also extremely limited. The operation of buses is noted in Chapter 3 and, whilst frequent buses unload from Zakynthos they are not permitted to pick up passengers who have not travelled from the islands. Although the drivers are sometimes open to persuasion, only the two daily buses to Patras provided by the local KTEL are officially available for passengers without their own vehicles.

Igoumenitsa

The principal port of north-western Greece is Igoumenitsa, very close to the border with Albania and at the end of the long overland route through the mountains from Andirrion, although the majority of traffic now travels over the wild mountains of Epirus to central and northern Greece and on to Turkey and the Middle East. Situated in a delightful bay and surrounded by mountains, it sees an increasing ferry traffic to all of the Italian ports on the Adriatic. Although traditionally an intermediate port of call for the larger ferries travelling to Patras, very considerable passenger and freight traffic now uses the port and the inflexibility caused by the unsophisticated port infrastructure means that vessels making intermediate calls are often in harbour for two hours or more loading and unloading their traffic. Here, perhaps more than anywhere else in Greece, a more sophisticated operation would provide enormous benefit to the shipping lines that use it. Indeed, it is the delays of using Igoumenitsa and

Right: *Locally built ferry Proteus arriving at Kilini from Zakynthos in 1990.*

Above: *Convincingly rebuilt from a ro-ro to a passenger ferry, the former **Breizh-Izel** seen as Marlines' **Duchess M** in 1995.*

Corfu that have opened the way to the express services now provided by Superfast and Minoan Lines, the Ancona service of the former operating non-stop from Patras.

Despite its extensive traffic, there is no standage space at all within the port for parking or marshalling vehicles for loading. The port is at its busiest in the early morning and evening, at which points in the day the town is full of vehicles jostling to reach ships which the drivers are unable to see (and may well not yet have arrived) while others relax in the middle of the highway in the knowledge that they have time to spare. While making the town a noisy and uncomfortable overnight stop, the daily theatre that this activity provides is not to be underestimated! Ultimately all the traffic will be embarked and the town will revert to relative peace for a few hours before the next group of ferries descend upon it.

Corfu

By the far the most attractive of the Adriatic ports, Corfu's harbour is on the eastern side of the island looking towards the Albanian mountains. Dark and empty at night and bleak and desolate by daytime, they form a wonderful backdrop for the ferries that pass through the Corfu Channel separating this green and relaxed holiday island from the wildness of Albania. In this narrow channel the Albanian government placed mines in the way of a Royal Navy exercise in 1946 which led to the deaths of 46 British

seamen and the crippling of two destroyers. It has taken until the late 1990s for the repercussions of this incident to be settled. Corfu has traditionally enjoyed a frequent service throughout the year by most of the shorter international services and many of the long-haul ones as well. The harbour is a little to the north of the main town and ferries entering from the south (and those of deeper draft coming from the north as well) sweep past a cliff top terrace which backs onto Greece's only permanent cricket pitch, a relic of the British occupation of the Ionian islands after the defeat of Napoleon. Regrettably the changes in the nature of Adriatic ferry operations have seen a decline in the vessels calling at Corfu in recent years on passage between Italy and the Greek mainland ports.

Right: *Following the arrival of the locally built **Myrtos** at the port of Kilini, an MAN bus of the Zakynthos KTEL discharges from her stern under the supervision of the immaculately turned out port police. (This vessel has since been withdrawn from service.)*

The Operators

Chapter 10

Access Ferries

A new operator in the Brindisi to Igoumenitsa service in 1999, the omission of calls at Corfu demonstrates that the company aims primarily at the transit trade to Turkey rather than the Greek holiday market. Sailing daily overnight from Italy on a ten-hour schedule, the single ship employed is the much-travelled *Hermes* which began life in 1962 as TT Line's first vessel *Nils Holgersson* on the Baltic route between Travemunde and Trelleborg. After previous service in the Mediterranean with the now-defunct Shipping Company of Ikaria and then Arkadia Lines she was acquired in 1998 by a company called Lions Ferries. Despite issuing a brochure advertising sailings that year she spent the summer laid-up at Keratsini near Piraeus and has now joined Access Ferries as their first vessel.

Adriatica

A part of the Italian state-owned Finmare group, Adriatica Di Navigazione S.P.A. provides an extensive network of services from Italy's Adriatic coast. With a unique and elegant livery of ginger hull, white superstructure and buff funnel topped with the red white and green colours of the Italian flag, the funnels retain an elegant moulded representation of the lion of St. Mark, the symbol of the Venetian empire from the middle ages. They provide a wonderful stereotype when arriving in a Greek port of Italian style and sophistication, but without making any appreciable impact on the Greek ferry market with non-Italian passengers. Blessed with regular new tonnage paid for by the Italian taxpayer, the company has found it hard to compete with either the development of faster ships by Greek companies in recent years or the proliferation of low cost summer operators sailing under flags of convenience and now concentrates its activities on operations to Albania and the former Yugoslavia.

In the mid 1990s Adriatica sailed three very similar vessels, *Palladio*, *Sansovino* and *Laurana* on daily services between Brindisi, Bari and Ancona and Patras with the *Egitto Express* sailing every ten days between Venice, Bari, Patras, Heraklion and Alexandria in Egypt. By 1999 this operation had shrunk to the *Laurana* and *Egitto Express* operating an overnight service on alternate days in the low season and daily between mid-June and mid-September between Brindisi, Corfu, Igoumenitsa and Patras. Their early morning arrivals in Corfu in each direction are punctuated by very Italian and very extensive use of the loud speaker system and the noise of prolific conversation from the deck passengers unlike any other ships in the service! In 1999 the *Laurana* was unexpectedly diverted to run between Bari and Durres in Albania and the Patras route reduced to alternate days only.

The *Egitto Express* was built in 1980 for Adriatica as the *Espresso Cagliari* in a class of originally elegant smaller

Right: *Originally the first* **Nils Holgersson** *of TT lines, the* **Samaina** *sailed for the Ikaria Shipping Company for many years before absorption by Arkadia Lines in the early 1990s. She has since passed out of their fleet and now sails in the colours of Access Ferries.*

27

Above: *A still early morning at Corfu as Adriatica's* **Laurana** *arrives from Patras on route to Brindisi.*

Right: *An earlier generation of Adriatica vessel, the* **Tiepolo** *arriving in Corfu in 1991 has since been withdrawn and now sails in the Red Sea as the* **Al Salam Taba 1**.

provides only 400 lane metres of freight accommodation, which limits the profitability of the route. She operates at the low service speed of seventeen knots, which contributes to the difficulty that Adriatica shares with other operators in competing with the recent fast Greek ferries, but in her case compounded by her recent building and high capital cost compared to the majority of operators on the Brindisi routes.

Agoudimos Lines

Heavily involved in operations from Rafina (see Chapter 13) Agoudimos operates one of the oldest vessels still in service on the Adriatic on a regular service running between April and October between Brindisi and Igoumenitsa. Operating daily in the high season, she is at the mainland port between nine and eleven each morning, although these timings change with the seasons.

The *Kapetan Alexandros A* is an example of a British-built ship which has been greatly improved in appearance as well as capacity after her sale to Greece. Built as the *Doric Ferry* for the Atlantic Steam Navigation's Transport Ferry Service in

ferries, an example of which can be seen in the Aegean as Ventouris Ferries' *Pegasus*. Originally providing accommodation for 395 cabin passengers and 440 deck passengers with 203 cars and only 400 lane metres of freight accommodation, she was very heavily and surprisingly attractively rebuilt in 1991 with enlarged forward superstructure and much other work for her service to Egypt. She now provides accommodation for 600 cabin passengers and 228 on deck; her car and freight capacity having been unaffected. Unlike her running mate she operates with a white hull which is excellently maintained by her Italian crew.

The stubby *Laurana*, built by Fincantieri in Ancona carries 1,094 passengers, of whom only 342 have cabin accommodation. Despite her beamy appearance, she also

Below: *The* **Laurana** *in the port of Corfu early in the morning in 1994.*

Above: *Originally ASN's Doric Ferry of 1962, Agoudimos Lines'* **Kapetan Alexandros** A *seen manoeuvring in the port of Corfu in 1995.*

1962 by the Ailsa Shipbuilding Company of Troon, she survived in the TFS fleet after its take-over by European Ferries in 1971 and subsequent absorption into the Townsend Thoresen operations and livery in 1976. She initially served on the Tilbury to Antwerp/Rotterdam services and her modest tonnage of 2,573 originally provided capacity for 35 passengers in some luxury and thirty lorries. Sold to Greece in 1981, she initially operated with few alterations as *Atlas II* before major rebuilding to provide additional cabins. After acquisition by Agoudimos Lines she operated initially from Rafina before transfer to the Adriatic in 1996. Although modifications have taken place to her engines since arrival in Greece which have increased her maximum speed to about sixteen knots, she provides one of the slower ways of crossing the Adriatic and even her relatively undemanding timetable can prove ambitious so that toward the end of her six day week she is sometimes to be found running up to twelve hours late. However, she has an undoubted niche in this market and it is to be hoped than this demonstration of an unusually early example of a classic ro-ro vessel will remain in service into the twenty-first century.

Anatolia Ferries

An operator in the expanding trade directly between Italy and the port of Çesme in Turkey, which can see up to six departures on summer Saturdays from Brindisi, Anatolia Ferries do not serve Greek ports but do operate the majority of their sailings through the Corinth Canal, one of the wonders of the Greek ferry system.

Much the older of the two vessels, the *Bosporos* sails from Brindisi on Saturday and Wednesday nights returning on Mondays and Fridays, with a large complement of passengers and their cars. Originally built in Belgium in 1962 as the *Koningin Fabiola*, a 22-knot car ferry with limited freight capacity which survived in the Belgian Marine/RMT fleet until withdrawal

Above: *Before purchase by Agoudimos Lines and conversion with extra superstructure and passenger accommodation, the* **Kapetan Alexandros A** *had a short spell as the* **Atlas II** *in which guise she is seen in 1981 little altered from her days with ASN.*

Above: *Although rebuilt at the stern and now flying the flag of St Vincent and the Grenadines, Anatolia Ferries'* **Bosporus** *remains recognisable as Belgian Marine's car ferry* **Koningin Fabiola** *of 1962. She is seen being inspected by a typical group of Turkish passengers at Brindisi's Outer Harbour in 1999 before departure to Çesme via the Corinth Canal.*

in 1983. Sold in 1985, she subsequently served with Hellenic Mediterranean Lines as their *Lydia* operating between Patras and Brindisi (and finally between Igoumenitsa and Otranto) until withdrawn in 1996. She has subsequently sailed under the colours of Topas Lines and Stern Lines before joining her current operators in 1998.

The other ship in the fleet is the *Jupiter* which began life at the Helsingør shipyard where she was built for DFDS as the *Surrey*, a ro-ro cargo vessel in the 'Butterboat' trade between Esbjerg and Grimsby. Initially quoted as providing 1,536 lane metres of cargo space for trailers, she served on most of the DFDS freight routes in the North Sea before being sold in 1992 to A.K. Ventouris. She was considerably rebuilt in Greece to provide additional passenger accommodation for 800 (of whom three quarters must endure long passages on deck) with little reduction in her cargo space. Sold by A.K. Ventouris after the 1996 season she spent 1997 with the short-lived Adria Ferries operating between Brindisi and Igoumenitsa before joining her current operators. She makes a single round trip between Brindisi and Çesme, leaving Italy late on Saturday nights, and following her return to Brindisi, runs for the rest of the week to Albania.

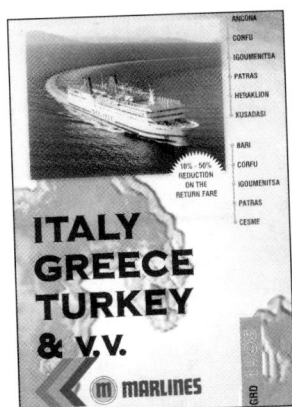

ANEK (The Shipping Company of Crete)

Based in Chania in western Crete, ANEK has had to work hard to emulate its rival Minoan Lines based in the capital of Crete, Heraklion. Although maintaining the unique distinction of sailing to Greece from the northern port of Trieste, it has found the increased competition from Ancona with the new ships of Superfast and Minoan hard to match with its former Japanese tonnage. The recent decision to order two new vessels to take advantage of the proceeds of the recent stock offering represents a somewhat belated effort to recapture a market in which the company once had a strong position.

The four vessels deployed in the Adriatic enjoyed considerable stability until the replacement of the *Talos,* which had served on the route since 1988 was transferred to LANE in 1999 (see Chapter 17) and replaced by the *Sophoklis V*, another former Japanese ferry acquired in 1998 and rebuilt in the following winter. Her twenty-five knot speed will give the possibility of improved competition over her rivals and, with accommodation for 1,925 lane metres of freight, she offers the largest capacity in the fleet. Her modern and very Japanese profile with a deep hull beneath a comparatively modest superstructure adds some style to a fleet which does not otherwise offer elegance to the eye. The second Greek ferry to carry the name of Sophoklis Venizelos, the post-war prime minister of Greece, albeit that his surname has been reduced to an initial V to avoid confusion with her larger fleetmate, she has little in common with her predecessor – better known as the early post-war Newhaven-Dieppe steamer *Londres*.

The two vessels deployed on the Ancona service since 1997 have been the large but hideous *Kriti I* and *Kriti II*, both built in Japan in 1979 and extensively rebuilt at the shipyards

Above: *One of a pair of lumbering sisters converted for ANEK in the mid 1990s, the **Kriti I** reverses slowly onto her berth at Igoumenitsa on her passage from Patras to Ancona – note the two crew members at the end of the stern ramp which is already horizontal some half kilometre away from the berth, and also the anchors ready to drop as she approaches the quay which will then be used to assist hauling her off at departure time.*

in Elefsis. Not particularly handy ships, their large freight capacity and space for deck passengers help to balance their heavy fuel consumption and apparent difficulty to maintain the 24-hour non-stop schedules which are demanded on some crossings. The pair provide a total of six weekly crossings in each direction between them, four of which call en route at Igoumenitsa where extensive business is done en route. They provide comfortable accommodation for 472 berthed passengers in a total complement of 1,600 as well as making very effective use of the 1,700 lane metres of freight space they offer. The two previous ferry ships to carry the name *Kriti* were also spectacularly ugly ships during their service in Greek waters. The first was originally Associated Humber Lines' *Melrose Abbey* of 1929 which served in the Typalados Fleet from 1959 until 1968 and more recently the Japanese vessel which now sails as the *Super Naias* for Agapitos Lines after long service with ANEK. The lovely island of Crete deserves a more elegant vessel to carry its name than these four have managed.

Perhaps the most interesting vessel in the fleet is the *El Venizelos* which takes her name from the Cretan politician Eleftherios Venizelos, Prime Minister of Greece in the early years of the twentieth century and architect of the union with the former Turkish provinces of northern Greece in 1912. The vessel formed part of a four ship order placed by Stena Line with the Gdansk shipyard in Poland in 1980. Two of the sisters were eventually completed in 1987 as the *Stena Scandinavica* and *Stena Germanica* and have since maintained the Gothenburg to Kiel service on which they currently continue. The third and fourth ships were cancelled by Stena in 1988 as uncompleted hulls and the first of these, originally intended to carry the name *Stena Polonica*, was

brought to Greece after various other parties had been involved and was subject to a lengthy rebuild in Perama, eventually being completed in 1992 some eight years after she was launched.

Unmistakably a close sister of her Scandinavian counterparts, she provides a fast and comfortable, if somewhat massive, presence on the Patras to Trieste service on which she provides two round trips per week. Her enormous height is inclined to dominate the ports in which she calls, particularly in Corfu where she is very much the largest ship to regularly call. Designed for drive through operation in Scandinavia, with separate side loading to her upper vehicle deck, she demonstrates most markedly the inflexibility of single deck loading through her comparatively narrow stern door and calls at the intermediate ports (particularly at Igoumenitsa) often comfortably exceed the two hour slots that the timetables provide.

The two ships due for delivery in 2000/1 are the first newbuildings for the company in its history and will be larger than any of the current fleet; measuring 30,000 tons and with 1,560 lane metres of freight capacity and a separate car deck for 150 vehicles and accommodation for 1,800 passengers. They have been ordered from the Norwegian Fosen shipyard but it has not been announced if both will join the Ancona service as has been widely anticipated. Their 27.5 knot service speed will help to enhance ANEK's position in the competitive market that the Adriatic now provides.

Traditionally operating with the air conditioning a little cooler than the passenger expects, the ships of ANEK provide an excellent demonstration of the splendid courtesy and reserve as well as marine competence of Cretan seafarers.

Although ANEK's operations are now centred exclusively on Ancona and Trieste, until 1997 the company also ran a daily service during the summer to Bari. The limitations of that port have been noted in Chapter 7 and the introduction of the large 'Kriti' ships on the Ancona service 1997 saw an end to this shorter route.

Above: *Currently the largest ship in ANEK's fleet, the El Venizelos arriving at Patras early one summer morning. Unmistakably a sister ship of Stena's Polish-built pair on the Gothenburg to Kiel service, she also betrays clear signs of the conversion carried out at Perama before entering service in Greece.*

Ascot Lines

Among the ebbing and flowing fortunes of the companies in the summer trade from Brindisi are operators who, with great enthusiasm, seize the chance to charter an elderly vessel or two. Although by no means all of them ever even commence their services, Ascot Lines operated in the late 1990s with an Igoumenitsa to Brindisi service operated by the *Thessalonika*. An interesting vessel, the first to sail for Prinz Line between Hamburg and Harwich as *Prinz Hamlet*, she later spent many years with DANE (see Chapter 17) as their *Kamiros*. She offers a slow but comfortable alternative to the modern vessels now increasingly taking over the Adriatic routes.

Catamaran Ferry Lines

Trading under this title, AT Cruises operated until 1995 with the small Belgian-built passenger catamaran *Manto*, a vessel which has the distinction of being the only craft registered in Ostend to operate in Greek waters but lacks much other attraction. In 1998 posters appeared in both Corfu and Athens indicating that she was shortly to re-enter the Igoumenitsa/Corfu/Brindisi trade, but the service did not materialise and its future is very much in question.

Corfu

The operation of the regular landing craft service between Corfu and Igoumenitsa is described in Chapter 8. Operated by a consortium of seven operators, including both Agapitos Lines and Agapitos Express Ferries, no less than thirteen landing craft ferries operate a basically hourly service taking, according to the age and condition of their engines, about ninety minutes for the passage. Engine maintenance has not always been matched by similar attention to the silencers of these vessels and travel on them can be an

Above: *The Belgian registered **Manto** of Catamaran Lines arriving in Corfu in 1994.*

almost literally deafening experience.

Dissatisfaction with the very basic facilities on these ferries has been a reason for the introduction of the two larger ferries by FEAX and Kerkyra Lines, but the simple equipment, small crew and low capital costs of these ships mean that they continue to dominate a market which fluctuates greatly with the holiday season but on which a generally consistent service is provided throughout the year. All the ships were built at Greek shipyards and are listed separately in the fleet list. Details of individual capacities have proved elusive, but vary between 600 and 800 passengers in summer, which is reduced by more than half during the winter season which can produce impressive storms in these narrow waters.

Cretan Ferries

The comparatively exposed open passages and lack of year round custom have meant that only one regular fast ferry service has operated in the Adriatic with any success while many others, usually employing ex-Russian Hydrofoils similar to those used by Flying Dolphins in the Aegean (see Chapter 17) have come and gone in the past fifteen years. The exception, rather unexpectedly run by Cretan Ferries based in Rethimnon in western Crete, has been the *Nearchos* – a Westamarin type W100D catamaran. She has a very small open deck area at the stern from which the delightful coastal scenery between Corfu, Paxos and Preveza can be seen on her morning run to Amphilochia, returning in the evening. The otherwise enclosed interior is not an obvious improvement in its environment on the Mercedes buses from Igoumenitsa with whom she has competed. However, she has not operated since 1997 and it seems likely that this operation will have gone the way of numerous other Greek fast ferry routes.

Diler Lines

Despite the continuing armed belligerence of Greece and Turkey, notwithstanding their shared membership of NATO, the summer of 1998 produced the remarkable novelty of this Turkish owned company taking up regular services between Brindisi, Corfu and Igoumenitsa. Aimed at the transit market of both passengers and freight heading for Turkey and on to the Middle East, daily overnight sailings from Italy have been made year-round. The ships employed are the *Captain Zaman I* and *II* and not the least remarkable feature is their registration in Belize City, whose marine surveyors no doubt enforce strict discipline on the maintenance and operation of the ships despite their great distance from them. The ships are, however, a delight. First in service was the *Captain Zaman II*, built in 1966 for Swedish Lloyd to operate between Hull and Gothenburg as the *Svea*, she is the author's nomination for the most elegant car ferry yet built. Externally scarcely altered since entering service over thirty years ago, she continued to serve Swedish Lloyd on the Southampton to Bilbao route as the *Hispania* and later as *Saga* on the Tilbury to Gothenburg service before being sold to Minoan Line in 1978 as their *Knossos*.

After regular service between Piraeus and Heraklion in Crete, she spent over a decade running on Minoan's Adriatic services from Patras to Venice, Ancona and a final season on the Brindisi to Corfu and Igoumenitsa triangle before being retired at the end of 1997 season. With her internal woodwork in cabins and public rooms, her classic profile and retaining her elegant white livery and maroon and green funnel she makes a dramatic contrast to the hideous products of Tokyo and Kobe that she passes on her regular daily services.

Extensively advertised amongst the Turkish community in northern Europe and in Turkey, she seemed to attract predictably little traffic from Greece but to carry good loads during the summer. In 1999 she has been joined by her sister *Captain Zaman I*, built for Swedish Lloyd as the *Saga* she opened the England Sweden Line joint service with Ellerman Wilson Lines between Hull and Gothenburg before being relieved by EWL's *Spero* (now NEL's *Sappho* – see Chapter 17) and inaugurating service between Tilbury and Gothenburg later in the year. Withdrawal in autumn 1971 was

Below: *Still in her former Minoan Lines livery, the **Captain Zaman II** of Diler Lines sailing from Corfu for Igoumenitsa during her first season in their fleet, newly registered in Belize but virtually unaltered from her original form as Swedish Lloyd's **Svea**.*

followed by an itinerant career including years sailing on the English Channel as *Olau Finn*, then joining Minoan Lines in 1987 as the *Fedra*. After service in both Adriatic and Aegean seas she was also sold in early 1998 to the Turkish company who promptly installed her on a route from Malta to Libya. Her charterer was the Libyan government who were attempting to overcome United Nations sanctions. Following the restoration of more normal trading with that country the elegant pair have been reunited. It is to be hoped that they will continue to sail for many years to come although they have not been repainted since their 1997 overhauls for Minoan and now present a somewhat shabby external appearance.

European Seaways

A Greek based operator who have included the one time Thoresen *Viking II*, later Sealink's *Earl William* (now the *Çesme Stern* of Stern Lines) in its fleet of fascinating older shipping, they have provided at least intermittent services from Brindisi to Igoumenitsa and Patras, but in

early 1998 sold the last vessel then in their fleet for service in the Black Sea. This did not deter them from issuing a 1998 brochure although they ultimately failed to operate. In 1999 they resumed service between Brindisi, Corfu and Igoumenitsa six times weekly with the unlovely *Ionis*.

Express Trailer Ferries

The only manifestation on the international routes in the Adriatic of the mushrooming empire in the Aegean established by Agapitos Express Ferries is the *Sea Trader*, a much travelled Japanese vessel running between Corinth (and occasionally Piraeus) and Venice. Although the vessel has considerable passenger accommodation and does carry some drivers, she is not currently in the normal passenger services on the Adriatic and appears to represent a toe in very competitive waters, which may lead to greater commitment in future.

Above: *Fragline's* **Ouranos** *arriving at Corfu on her daily cycle between Brindisi, Corfu and Igoumenitsa. She was withdrawn from service at the end of the 1998 season.*

Feax Express Lines

A new operator in 1998 in the Igoumenitsa to Corfu service, this company has introduced by far the largest and most comfortable vessel in this busy service. Operating in collaboration (but with no apparent common ownership) with Kerkyra Lines (see below), the two companies offer a total of six sailings in each direction per day, with one ship making seven single journeys and the other five on alternating rosters.

Re-equipped with a pointed bow, a forward bridge and substantial superstructure it is hard to recognise the *Pantokrator* as the former double ended ferry *Superflex Foxtrot*, built by North-East Shipbuilders Limited in Sunderland in 1988 and little used her original form. She was substantially rebuilt on Salamis over the years 1995 to 1997 and is clearly a matter of considerable pride to her owners and crew. Whether the government regulated fares can support this level of sophistication remains to be seen, but it is very apparent that regular travellers time their journeys to use this handsome vessel in preference to the noisier and considerably slower opposition.

Her rebuilding included replacing the deck-top engines in containers which were a feature of the original Superflex design with a proper engine room containing two MAN diesels.

Five Stars Lines

Formed in early 1999 following the dissolution of the partnership behind Med Link Lines (see below), this company has entered the Brindisi to Patras trade with the hideous *Poseidon*. Originally the Japanese *Suzuran Maru*, she came to Greece in 1994. She is no doubt a profitable ship with considerable capacity but she does little to grace the harbours she visits. She operates on alternate days between Brindisi and Patras via Igoumenitsa.

Fragline

After fifteen years of operating a pair of ships between Brindisi, Corfu, Igoumenitsa and Patras, the operation was halved in size and length of service in 1995 when the former *Eolos* was sold to A.K. Ventouris, for whom she has subsequently sailed as *Agios Vassilios* (see below). The company continue using only a single ship running a daily triangular service between Brindisi, Corfu and Igoumenitsa.

Although a dated ship by modern standards, the *Ouranos* provided a remarkably consistent service over a long season between mid March and late October with notable reliability. Originally built for a service in Norway, she subsequently spent four years on the North Sea service of Prinz Ferries between Hamburg and Harwich as the second *Prinz Hamlet* and a further twelve years running between Spain and Morocco as the *Agadir* before joining Fragline service in 1986. Although her facilities were considerably restricted when compared to the more recent vessels that she competed with, her fares were 25% lower than their prices and she carried consistently good loadings. Laid-up at the end of her 1998 season she has since been sold for further service in the Azores.

Her replacement is yet another elegant ship with an

Below: *Her replacement with Fragline in 1999 and only partially repainted from her previous Minoan Lines livery, the* **Ouranos** *seen loading at Brindisi for her evening sailing to Corfu and Igoumenitsa was originally Tor Line's* **Tor Hollandia** *before 22 years' service as the* **Ariadne** *on Minoan's Adriatic and Aegean services.*

interesting history and has taken over the name *Ouranos* from her predecessor. Built in 1967 as the *Tor Hollandia* for the introduction of passenger services between Immingham, Amsterdam and Gothenburg by Tor Line, she was replaced in 1976 on North Sea services by the *Tor Britannia* and *Tor Scandinavia* (now DFDS Seaways *Prince of Scandinavia* and *Princess of Scandinavia*). She was brought to the Mediterranean by Minoan Lines as their first modern ship *Ariadne* for their original service between Piraeus and Heraklion, the capital of Crete. A comfortable ship with a good freight capacity for her time, she later worked on most services of Minoan Lines including a couple of seasons in the

Above: *Afternoon in Brindisi as Hellenic Mediterranean Lines'* **Media II** *(originally Thoresen's* **Viking I**) *arrives from Patras as Agoudimos Line's* **Kapetan Alexandros A** *(originally ASN's* **Doric Ferry**) *loads for Corfu and Igoumenitsa.*

early 1990s on an interesting route between Italy and Turkey via Patras, the Corinth Canal and Piraeus. After spending two subsequent seasons sailing on Minoan's service from Piraeus to the Cyclades, she was sold in early 1999 to Fragline to replace the earlier *Ouranos*. Externally only her funnels were repainted from her previous livery and the 1999 brochure continued to illustrate the previous ship – it is entirely possible that she will herself soon be replaced by a newer vessel.

Hellenic Mediterranean Lines

Established in 1939 and operating an extensive fleet of 39 passenger ships by the time of the German invasion in 1941, Hellenic Mediterranean Lines emerged as the Greek national flag carrier on the Adriatic. In recent times progressively starved of capital investment by political pressure on its government owners it has survived due to the

Above: *The* **Lydia**, *little altered from her days on the English Channel, at sea off Albania.*

Below: *The first purpose-built car ferry in Greece, HML's* **Egnatia** *of 1960 seen in her final season in 1995 arriving at Corfu.*

Above: *Externally unaltered from her days as Irish Ferries'* **Saint Patrick II**, *the* **Egnatia II** *now sails in the elegant livery of Hellenic Mediterranean Lines. She is seen in Brindisi's Inner Harbour loading for the Greek ports of Igoumenitsa, Kefalonia and Patras.*

determination of its managers. A lucrative contract to carry the holders of Inter Rail tickets between Brindisi and Patras combined with an excellent network of ticket sales offices has seen the service continue and recently the introduction of the Irish Ferries vessel *Saint Patrick II* has brought at least some life back into the operation.

The company had the distinction to operate the *Egnatia*, the first purpose built Greek car ferry, delivered from Le Havre in 1960 to open a daily car service in co-operation with Adriatica's *Appia*. The pioneer vessel was taken out of service in 1995, but remains laid-up at Elefsis and appears to remain in excellent condition. Her withdrawal was precipitated by reaching the thirty-five year time limit on service of Greek registered ships and further political pressure making a transfer to a flag of convenience impractical.

The company entered the 1990s with a fleet of seven vessels, five of which have served British ports for large portions of their earlier careers. These included not only the immensely elegant *Lydia*, the one time Belgian Marine *Koningin Fabiola* and now serving with Anatolia Ferries, but also Europe's last working turbine steam ship, the *Corinthia*, originally British Railways' *Duke of Argyll* of the Heysham-Belfast service. She remained in operation until 1993, but the ending of her era still left the former Belfast Steamship Company twins *Ulster Prince* and *Ulster Queen* in service as the *Neptunia* (later *Panther*) and *Poseidonia* respectively. These were balanced by the original *Travemunde* and the ex-Thoresen *Viking I* sailing in tandem as the *Apollonia II* and *Media II* respectively.

However, the onset of tighter safety regulations for old ships and a further cut in the government's financial support led to a further reduction in operations with only the former

Saint Patrick II sailing as the *Egnatia II* and the ex-Thoresen ship running on a complicated roster between Brindisi and Patras via Corfu, Igoumenitsa, Kefalonia, Zakynthos in varying combinations according to day and season.

It is to be hoped that this interesting fleet in their elegant delivery of grey hulls and yellow funnels with a blue hoop near the top will enjoy a revival which will enable the company to continue to serve for many years to come.

Jadrolinija

The Croatian state-owned shipping line operates around forty ships in its services along the Croatian coast and across the Adriatic to Italy. Currently one sailing per week of the coastal service is continued from Dubrovnik via Bari to Igoumenitsa, arriving on Mondays in high summer and Fridays the rest of the year. The ship spends the day in the Greek port before returning northwards in the evening on one of the most interesting routes in the Adriatic via Dubrovnik and Split to Rijeka.

The ships used on the route are interesting too. The regular summer vessel is the *Marko Polo*, which has been with the Croatian company since 1988. She began life in 1973 at Le Havre, where she was built for Larvik Line as their *Peter Wessel*. After eleven years on the Skagerrak running between northern Denmark and southern Norway, she spent two years with the Dutch Zeeland Steamship Company as their *Zeeland* on the route from Hook of Holland to Harwich and then had a short spell with Stena before coming to Yugoslavia in 1988. Initially operating with a communist red star on her funnel, this was given way to the more recent 'J' logo of her post communist operators.

Her running mate on the Greek route is the *Dubrovnik*,

Above: *The elegant **Marko Polo** of Jadrolinija picking up her anchor as she sails from Igoumenitsa for Bari, Dubrovnik and Split on a summer evening in 1998.*

built at Cork in 1979 for B & I Line as the *Connacht* for the Cork to Swansea and Pembroke Dock services. She subsequently operated between Dublin and Liverpool (and later Holyhead) before sale in 1988 to Brittany Ferries who extensively refurbished her as the *Duchesse Anne*. After

serving on the majority of their routes she was rendered surplus after the 1996 season and moved to the Adriatic. She continues to present an extremely trim profile, scarcely altered for her new trade.

Jadrolinija continue to operate a number of other ferries

Above: *Marlines' **Crown M** seen off Corfu was little altered from her days as the Bergen Line/Fred. Olsen **Jupiter**.*

Above: *Another one-time British vessel which served with Marlines, **Baroness M** seen at Izmir in Turkey on the long route from Bari via Patras in 1986 showing the additional superstructure added after her transfer to Greece. Originally built for Irish Sea services as the **Lion**, she later operated on P&O's Dover to Boulogne service.*

Below: *The distinctive lines of P&O's **Leopard** of 1967 seen in the livery of Marlines as the **Countess M**. Note the short forward sun deck and additional rear superstructure added after sale to Greece.*

which have in past years sailed to Corfu, Igoumenitsa and Patras but it seems likely that the promised expansion of their services in future years will be met by the acquisition of further new and interesting tonnage.

Kerkyra Lines

A small Japanese-built car ferry was bought by a Corfu based company in 1994 to operate the first serious competition with the landing craft ferries. Her operations are now co-ordinated with more recent operations of Feax Express Lines noted above. Named *Agios Spiridon* after the patron saint of Corfu whose mummified body is displayed in the island cathedral, she is more spacious and a better sea boat than the landing craft, but her Daihatsu engines liberally coat the decks with an oily residue which impregnates her passengers seeking relief on deck from the noisy throbs within.

Marlines

This privately owned company, belonging to the Marangopolos family, have operated a fascinating collection of ships through the 1990s, all but one of

which have served in British waters. Founded in 1982, they operated until 1997 between Ancona, Igoumenitsa and Patras as well as a long distance service between Ancona and Çesme in Turkey but have since retreated to the Bari to Igoumenitsa line with only two ships in operation in 1999. A lack of the capital required for fleet renewal and an increasingly elderly and slow fleet have led to the laying up of the majority of the ships and the sale of others to Black Sea operators in 1998. Services have recently been operated by the *Duchess M*, heavily rebuilt from a freight ro-ro originally constructed in Hong Kong for service in New Zealand and later operated by Brittany Ferries and then British Channel Island Ferries as *Breizh Izel*. The extraordinary, but successful, conversion carried out at Perama has produced a vessel which is both relatively handsome and with adequate capacity for summer loads on this inexpensive route.

During spring and autumn she is replaced by the considerably larger *Dame M*, a Japanese ro-ro freighter extensively rebuilt at Perama during the early 1990s as an elegant ferry with much passenger accommodation above

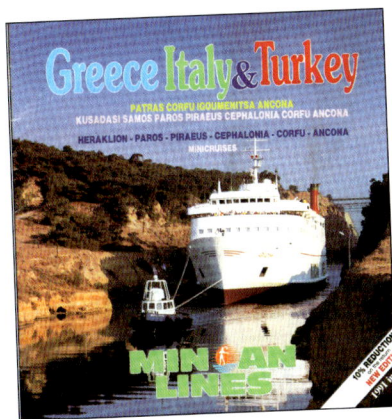

Right: *Splendidly rebuilt in Greece from previous service as a Japanese ro-ro, the **Dame M** seen off the coast of Albania in 1995.*

the vehicle decks. She has spent three summer seasons on charter to the Tunisian operator Cotunav, but has returned to Greece for the remainder of the year. Fully compliant with current Solas requirements, she probably has the longest future of the ships in this fleet. Her sister ship, intended to carry the name *Grace M* but never rebuilt, has spent six years laid-up at Elefsis and it seems improbably that she will ever enter the fleet.

The other vessel in regular Adriatic service is the *Countess M*, originally built as Normandy Ferries' *Leopard* for service from Southampton to Le Havre in 1967 and only withdrawn after spending the 1985 season in Townsend Thoresen livery. She came to Greece in 1986 and was extensively rebuilt with a small forward balcony at the end of the promenade deck and considerable additional cabins at the stern. Her sister *Dragon* was also briefly in the Marlines fleet firstly as *Viscountess M*, later renamed as *Charm M* before sale to the Black Sea in 1997.

Now laid-up and swinging alone on a buoy off Elefsis is the *Crown M*, scarcely rebuilt externally since her introduction to service in 1966 as the Bergen Line/Fred Olsen vessel *Jupiter* for the Newcastle to Bergen summer service, spending her winters on the cruise ferry route from London to the Canary Islands. She was sold to her current owner in 1990 and has seen extensive service in the Adriatic, for which she is well suited with the swimming pool and other luxury facilities provided at the time of her building. A return to service seems entirely possible.

Med Link Lines

Sailing between Brindisi, Igoumenitsa, Kefalonia and Patras, Med Link Lines have operated since 1993 with some extremely assorted ships. In addition they run a twice-weekly route between Brindisi, Patras and Turkey using the Corinth Canal. They operate year-round with an extensive freight traffic in collaboration with Italian handling agents and provide a successful competitor to the larger companies with their interesting fleet.

Above: *One of five Greek ferries to have sailed under the white ensign, the* **Agios Andreas** *seen at Patras after rebuilding following service as HMAS* **Jervis Bay** *– she was originally built as the* **Australian Trader**.

The oldest of the current vessels is the *Afrodite II* built in 1967 at Swan Hunter on the Tyne for ASN's Transport Ferry Service as their *Europic Ferry*. After long service with ASN and subsequently Townsend Thoresen, she was requisitioned in 1982 to join the British Task Force sent to recapture the Falkland Islands from Argentina. Having entered San Carlos Water in the company of the P & O Liner *Canberra* on the first day of the landings, she was repeatedly attacked by the Argentinean Air Force and for the remainder of her service with Townsend Thoresen and later P & O proudly displayed in her dining room the naval battle honour awarded to her for this service. Finally displaced from the Cairnryan to Larne service in 1992, she has had considerable additional deck space created on the aft part of the ship. She represented the first major attempt on the Adriatic to provide 'camp on board' facilities for the many Italian and German holidaymakers travelling in caravans. Now widely copied by ANEK, Minoan, Strintzis and Ventouris Ferries, it enables the passengers to live in the same standard of accommodation that they will

Above: *The first of a flood of newbuildings for Minoan Lines in the 1990s, the* **Aretousa** *demonstrating the high speed branding on her hull.*

Above: *Only the after superstructure has been greatly altered since her days as Atlantic Steam Navigation's* **Europic Ferry** *but the appearance of the ship is vastly different as Med Link Lines'* **Afrodite II** *arrives at Patras from Brindisi in the summer of 1994.*

'enjoy' for the remainder of their holiday while paying only a deck class fare rather than for cabin accommodation on board ship. The principal difference in use of the accommodation are the strictly announced (and one hopes enforced) regulation against using gas cooking on board and the opportunity to sleep inches away from a swaying container lorry. Unattractive as this sounds, it is as nothing compared to the visual assault which was inflicted upon this fine ship at Perama when the conversion was carried out with curiously shaped holes constructed in the new superstructure. At least they provide some light and air to the unfortunate campers.

Her regular running mate between Brindisi, Igoumenitsa and Patras arrived from Japan in 1998 following the transfer of the hideous *Poseidon* to Five Stars Lines. The *Maria G* has been considerably rebuilt from her earlier service as the Japanese day ferry *Okudogo 3* and provides a whole deck for her wretched campers on board with a single deck of cabins perched above them and a substantial deck for freight below.

The regular vessel on the twice-weekly service from Brindisi to Çesme in Turkey is the *Agios Andreas*, named after the apostle whose head is venerated in the cathedral at

Top Right: *The elegant* **Captain Zaman I** *of Diler Lines was originally Swedish Lloyd's* **Saga** *and has had an itinerant career including eleven years with Minoan Lines as their* **Festos**. *She was photographed in 1999 sailing from the Italian port of Brindisi.*

Right: *Minoan Lines'* **Fedra** *sailing from Corfu in the morning sun.*

Above: *The long and very Japanese* **Erotokritos** *of Minoan Lines loading at Patras for Venice.*

Patras. She began her career as the *Australian Trader* sailing for Australian National Line between Melbourne and Northern Tasmania. An early example of what has since become known as a ro-pax, she did not prove the ideal combination and after eight years was sold to the Royal Australian Navy as HMAS *Jervis Bay* and served as a naval training ship from 1977 until sold to her current operators in 1994. Her superstructure was again extended at the stern, this time producing a relatively attractive vessel, sharing with her fleet mates considerable scope for camping on board.

Minoan Lines

The biggest and arguably the best of the lines sailing on the Adriatic, Minoan entered the Greece-Italy trade in 1981 with a single ship operation using the *El Greco* (now sailing between Thessalonika and Heraklion – see Chapter 17) but they have progressively expanded and invested in new ships. By 1991 Minoan were operating five times a week between Patras, Corfu, Igoumenitsa and Ancona with an interesting additional service between Heraklion, Piraeus, Kefalonia, Corfu and Ancona passing through the Corinth Canal. Sadly this opportunity is no longer available, but the company's operations have since expanded considerably and now provide daily departures between Patras, Igoumenitsa, Corfu and Venice while two newly built vessels operate an express service in twenty hours from Patras to Ancona via Igoumenitsa.

The company enjoys a high reputation for the standard of service on board and reliability, the crews remain largely Cretan in origin with some from other Aegean Islands. The naming of Minoan's ships is based on mythological figures and ancient sites of Minoan civilisation reflecting the company's roots in Crete.

Top right: *The* **Ikarus** *on her berth at Patras displaying the enormous stern doors required to achieve a rapid turnaround on the long service to Ancona.*

Right: *The Dutch-built Catamaran* **High Speed I** *of Minoan Lines seen at Piraeus before transfer to the Adriatic to operate between Patras and Corfu.*

For over a decade until the 1997 season it was possible to travel slowly and in considerable comfort in the beautiful ships *Knossos* and *Festos*, the former Swedish Lloyd twins now sold to Diler Lines. Despite their departure, the Minoan fleet retains a good variety of ships originating in northern Europe and Japan and an increasing quantity of newbuilding including a pair of large vessels now being built in the Far East to begin the re-equipment of the Venice service with the option of others to follow.

At present the Venice service is in the hands of an unusual assortment of the recent Norwegian-built *Aretousa*,

the increasingly elderly mid-sized Japanese vessel *Daedalus*, the German *Fedra* and the large Japanese ro-pax *Erotokritos* Despite their widely differing styles of accommodation and freight capacity, they enjoyed extremely successful 1998 and 1999 seasons and a similar deployment is expected to continue until the new South Korean ships arrive in 2001.

The *Aretousa* was the first ship to be built for Minoan in its history. Although emblazoned along her sides with the 'High Speed' legend which is applied to the faster ships on the Ancona route and to the catamaran operating from in the Aegean, her specified speed at 23.8 knots is not greatly in excess of standard Mediterranean speeds. She did however, introduce a new style and modernity into the service and has remained a popular and profitable unit in the fleet despite the newer and faster vessels that have since been acquired and ordered. Her hull was built at Landskrona in Sweden and mechanically and internally fitted out at the Fosen yard in north Norway. Her journey south in 1995 has brought her to a very different climate to which she is well adapted, with her upper vehicle deck being largely given over to camping on board (described above in the Med Link Lines section).

Remarkably elegant for a Japanese-built ship, *Daedalus* dates from 1973 and is noted for her comfortable passenger cabins. She will be replaced by one of the new South Korean ships in 2001 as will the *Fedra*, which joined the Minoan fleet in 1987, two years after her Japanese running mate. She offers a considerable passenger capacity of 1,800, but contains many small and cramped cabins, which have seen little alteration or updating from her original service between Travemunde and Trelleborg which she entered in 1974. The fourth member of the current Venice quartet is the 188 metre long *Erotokritos*, a sister of ANEK's *Lato* now running between Piraeus and Heraklion (see Chapter 17). Although her appearance has been improved by the removal of the side ramps still to be found on the ANEK ship, she is not a thing of beauty and in the course of her career the conversions have led to too many of her cabins being placed beneath

open decks with resulting disturbance to the passengers travelling in them. She does, however, provide an impressive grandstand from which to watch the city of Venice as she steams out into the Adriatic and has entirely adequate facilities as well as substantial capacity for camping on board.

From 1998 the Ancona service has been handled by two new ships, again built by Fosen. The *Ikarus* entered service in early 1998 and her 26.5-knot service speed has made the twenty-hour schedule, including the Igoumenitsa call, practical although difficult to achieve due to delays at the intermediate port. The comfortably furnished sisters are clearly winning back market share from Superfast Ferries, but the process was badly disrupted by the collision sustained by the *Pasiphae* on her maiden commercial sailing on 5th July 1998. She ran onto a reef near Corfu and required three weeks in a shipyard at Perama before being able to restart her sailings. Although some traffic was saved by the diversion of ships on the Venice route to fill up such spare capacity as they had at Ancona, it has caused a loss of goodwill and trade which is taking time to rebuild. The two sister ships again feature extensive vehicle capacity, including further 'camp on board' facilities and very comfortable cabins.

In 2000 Minoan are to transfer their only fast craft, the *High Speed I* to a new domestic route in the Adriatic. The acquisition of a new licence for her service from Patras to Corfu with calls at Kefalonia and Igoumenitsa has introduced a new element to the passenger services in the Adriatic. Whether she will manage to produce a good return on her investment on a route previously served by intermediate calls on international services will remain to be seen but she certainly opens new possibilities in generally predictable pattern of traffic.

The next development of Minoan's service is expected to be the delivery of the South Korean newbuildings for the Venice route. It is clear that the twenty-five knot service speed that has been specified with considerable freight capacity in a ro-pax arrangement (but still accommodating 1,500 passengers) will give the scope for a significant upgrade on the Venice service. The final deployment of these two vessels will be a matter of interest as the delivery dates near, currently anticipated for February and July 2001. If they do indeed serve Venice they are advertised to achieve a 21-hour crossing to Patras without intermediate calls. It is to be hoped that such a development will lead to the establishment of independent services by the company to Corfu and Igoumenitsa. The current diversion of the Ancona ships causes considerable disturbance to the Ancona service which does not help the competition with Superfast and the use of the *Aretousa* and the *Erotokritos* on such a route seems entirely possible.

With Minoan's current dominant position in the Adriatic, it is worth remembering that during 1995 and 1996 it formed part of a joint pool with Strintzis Lines. There was never a formal merger and the identities of the two companies and their agents was never compromised, but the alliance neither attracted the imagination of their customers nor did it

Top left: *The SES (surface effect ship)* **Santa Eleonora** *of Misano Alta Velocita arriving in Corfu on her daily service from Paxos to Brindisi in 1998.*

Left: *The Japanese-built* **Lady Terry** *of Poseidon Lines arriving in Corfu in 1991. After later service in the eastern Mediterranean, her operators have returned her to the Adriatic for the 1999 summer service.*

provide very convincing competition to the newly arrived Superfast Ferries. In those days while the Minoan ships could manage a 24-hour crossing (in competition to Superfast's twenty hours) the best that Strintzis fastest ship on the route (*Ionian Star* – since sold) could manage was 28 hours. After two years the joint operation was brought to an end by both partners who were able to resume their earlier competition, at which Minoan re-established its earlier dominant position.

Misano Alta Velocita Lines (Italian Ferries)

This Italian company has operated in the Paxos, Corfu and Brindisi service since 1993 and the operation continues as a fast and expensive way of transporting passengers to and from the holiday islands between April and September. With fares up to four times those of the conventional ferries it is little surprise that the sailings often run lightly loaded, but a crossing time of two and a quarter hours contrasts with ten hours or more on some of the slower conventional ships.

The *Santa Eleonora*, which operates the route, is a Surface Effect Ship built in Norway offering both first and economy class passage. Her noise and forty knot speed provide an interesting diversion in the morning ferry services from Corfu, but seem unlikely to provide a precedent for major expansion elsewhere. She usually spends her winters laid-up but her operators propose to deploy her in the future on a Brindisi to Valona route; whether the demand exists for such a service to central Albania must be a matter for speculation.

Petrakis Shipping Company

Even by the standards of Greek ship owners the fleet of this Corfu based operator is an unusual one, consisting of the four former Royal Navy wooden-hulled inshore minesweepers – H.M. Ships *Halsham*, *Sandringham*, *Thakeham* and *Thatcham*. Subsequent investigations have been unable to determine the former identities of the four ships which now sail under the names of *Petrakis*, *Petrakis I*, *Sotirakis* and *Sotirakis I* on daily services from Corfu to Paxos and, most interestingly, to Sarande in Albania. Their previous Bofors and Oerlikon guns and their minesweeping equipment having been removed to provide featureless accommodation for two hundred passengers who are treated to spectacular passages through the coastal waters of Corfu. Arrival in Albania on one of these modestly sized and equipped vessels will leave the traveller amazed at the deprivations that this wild country and wilder governments have forced upon its unhappy people.

All four vessels spent between eight and ten of the early years of their lives in mothballs and afterwards saw only very limited service before being sold at scrap prices by the Royal Navy but represent unexpected examples of British built ships in this corner of the Mediterranean.

Poseidon Lines

Although regular performers on the Adriatic through the 1990s, the pair of former Japanese ships operated by Poseidon Lines have suffered particular pressure from the increase in competition in the second half of the decade and did not operate in 1997 or 1998, although their eastern Mediterranean operations continued. This interesting and inexpensive operator re-established itself in 1999 in a daily service between Bari and Igoumenitsa again aimed mainly at the transit traffic to Turkey.

Preveza

An example of the efficiency of Greek ferry operations,

Above: *Rainbow Lines ro-ro line* **Niobe 1** *at sea off the Albanian port of Sarande in the summer of 1998.*

the five-minute passage over the mouth of the Ambracian Gulf from Preveza to Action is provided in a very Greek way. Five landing craft loading only over the bow make the short crossing. This is the only Greek ferry route which faces replacement by a fixed link; it will be superseded by a new tunnel to be built as part of a general upgrading of the road along the west coast of Greece.

Rainbow Lines

An exclusively freight operator running between Igoumenitsa and Bari which also provides an Italy to Albania passenger service, the fleet is one of the more unusual of those now in service in Greece. Built in 1969 in Le Havre for SNCF originally to run between Felixstowe and Dunkerque, the uninspiringly named *Transcontainer I* introduced the modern style of freight roll on-roll off ferries to the Straits of Dover when she subsequently entered service on the Dover to Dunkerque train ferry service. Her exceptional passenger accommodation for freight drivers was not matched with much capacity for either rail or road vehicles. After increasingly irregular service to Dover, Harwich, Felixstowe and Portsmouth, she was sold for service in the Red Sea. Subsequently rebuilt as the *Nour I* to operate between Nuweiba in Egypt and Aqaba in Jordan, she was rebuilt with enlarged passenger accommodation, allegedly for 1,000 passengers. She was soon transferred to freight service in the Adriatic and, although in 1998 the name of her operator was removed the hull, the *Niobe I* maintains an interesting and apparently profitable service in this most competitive of

Above: *A typically bustling scene at Andirrion as KTEL Mercedes buses are loaded onto the last few square metres of a landing craft waiting to cross the Gulf of Corinth.*

Above: *Seen at Igoumenitsa in 1995 as the **Pearl William** while in use on freight service, the former **Viking II** has had an eventful career. Withdrawn by Townsend Thoresen in 1976 after 13 years' service, she later served the Channel Islands under the Sealink flag as their **Earl William**. Sold in 1992 to Greece and subsequently resold and renamed on several occasions, she most recently sailed for Stern Lines as **Çesme Stern** but has since been laid-up.*

trades. Her running mate is the *Artemis I*, built in 1965 as the *Prinsessan Desiree* for service on the Kattegat but since heavily rebuilt – she normally operates from Bari to Albania.

Rion – Andirrion

While lacking the size and ostentation of the vessels on the services to Italy which berth at Patras, eight kilometres to the west, the seventeen landing craft operating from the sloping shores at Rion provide one of the busiest and most efficient ferry services in Europe. Crossing the three kilometre wide entrance to the Gulf of Corinth in twenty minutes, they provide a link between the National Road, a dual carriageway toll road from Athens along the south coast of the Gulf, and the fan of roads spreading north from the northern point of Andirrion. The mountains of Boeotia continue to provide a barrier which has yet to be breached by road-builders other than by continuously twisting steep routes unsuitable for heavy vehicles. As a result, an enormous traffic from much of North Western Greece must travel by this ferry to reach the main industrial and population centres of the country.

Although foot passengers are carried, the vessels rapidly fill with the Mercedes buses of the northern KTELs and heavy lorries as well as a mass of private cars and at busy times up to four ferries may be loading and unloading beside each other. At first sight the swirling traffic appears to be disorganised and dangerous but in reality the underlying patience and understanding of Greek motorists will lead those unfamiliar with the arrangements swiftly away.

The details of the vessels have proved elusive to discover but each carries approximately 75 cars or the equivalent in larger vehicles with a modest superstructure at the stern. Providing a brief respite from the roads, they offer a single cafeteria and some of the most continuously occupied lavatories afloat. The views of the surrounding mountains are quite magnificent and the efficiency of the service is wonderful to behold.

Sea Containers

The international transport empire established by the American James Sherwood and controlled from its ostentatious offices on London's South Bank has expressed interest in acquiring Turkish Maritime Lines when privatised. Within the published proposals for the development of services is the proposed introduction of one of the 'Super Sea Cat' class of vessels on a fifteen-hour service from Brindisi to Turkey via Patras and the Corinth Canal. Fitting neither into the cruise ferry market nor the extremely cheap style of transit favoured by the returning Turkish labourers and their families, it will be necessary to establish a totally new niche in a crowded market if the proposed operation is to succeed.

Stern Lines

Although not in operation in 1999, Stern Lines have recently operated two intriguing vessels on a regular service

Above: *The Australian-built **Ionian Bridge** displaying her boxy superstructure at Corfu on the service from Brindisi.*

Above: *The **Ionian Sun** sailing from Kilini was originally B&I Line's **Leinster**.*

through the Corinth Canal. Both came to the company after long service in other parts of the Greek ferry network and distinguished earlier careers in the English Channel. They operated a 36-hour crossing carrying passengers in summer and at least a limited quantity of freight during a longer season between Bari and Çesme on Turkey's Aegean coast.

The *Bosporos* now sails for Anatolia Ferries while her former fleetmate the *Çesme Stern* is laid-up in the port of Bari. Introduced in 1964 by Thoresen Car Ferries in the first year of their operations from Southampton to Cherbourg and Le Havre, she remained on the English Channel after sale to British Rail as the *Earl William* operating to the Channel Islands from Portsmouth and Weymouth until her sale in 1992. She has since operated for a variety of Adriatic and Eastern Mediterranean operators including European Seaways and in 1997 as the Turkish controlled *Mar-Julia* on the Brindisi to Igoumenitsa route. 1998 was spent operating with Stern Lines but, although there appears to be plenty of life left in her yet, she did not sail in 1999.

Strintzis Lines

One of the largest of the Greek shipping businesses, with substantial operations on both Adriatic and Aegean routes, Strintzis has a history of sailing a fascinating mixture of former northern European and Japanese ships as well as locally built ones. Still managed by the Strintzis family which founded the fleet in 1897, the company entered Adriatic traffic in 1977 and continued to grow, enabling it to become the first Greek ferry group to be listed on the Athens Stock Exchange. After operating in 1995/6 in a consortium with Minoan Lines on the Adriatic routes, Strintzis re-established its independent operations in 1997 and has since engaged in a spate of second-hand purchases and has subsequently placed orders for newbuildings in both Holland, South Korea and Greece. Having at one point appeared to be slipping into

the back waters on the Adriatic, this extensive investment will soon re-establish the company in the forefront of operators, but its available vessels in 1999 left it lagging somewhat behind its competitors.

After the withdrawal of the *Delos* (the former Newhaven-Dieppe vessel *Villandry*) in 1996 and her subsequent disposal for breaking in India, the oldest and in many ways the most interesting of the vessels in the current fleet is her sister *Eptanisos*, originally SNCF's *Valençay* from the same route, sold to Strintzis in 1984. Taking her current name from the Ionian Islands that she served during her first spell in cross-Adriatic service, she then operated for the first half of the 1990s on the Aegean routes from Rafina before returning for what will doubtless be her last spell of service, running in the Adriatic from Kilini to the island of Kefalonia in collaboration with her fleetmate of that name which operates from Patras – and in 1999 with the *Ionian Sun*. Little altered externally from her days at Dieppe except for a small extension at her stern, she remains a fast and popular (if somewhat noisy) vessel

Above: *Little altered from her service between Newhaven and Dieppe as the **Valençay**, Strintzis' **Eptanisos** arriving at Kilini from Kefalonia in 1998.*

Above: *The **Kefalonia** loading at Patras.*

with both the holiday makers who fill her upper decks in summer and the transport businesses who fill her vehicle deck year round. She is due to be replaced in the year 2000 and her age suggests that 1999 will be her last full season in the Greek register. She remains a tribute to those who built her in Saint Nazaire and who have sailed her subsequently, not least her Greek engineers who have served on her for the last fifteen years of her career.

The *Ionian Sun* returned to Adriatic waters in 1999 to share services from Kilini with the French-built ship, thirty years after her building at the Verolme shipyard in Cook as the B&I car ferry *Leinster*. Renamed in 1980 as the *Innisfallen*, she served on both the Dublin and Cork routes of the Irish company before coming to Greece in 1986. She has subsequently sailed on most of Strintzis Lines' routes from which she has been progressively ousted by larger tonnage. In the mid-90s she ran a Brindisi / Corfu / Igoumenitsa service for which her speed was not quite adequate and spent 1998 on a roster which effectively duplicated the sailings of the *Superferry II* from Rafina. She even had a memorable 1990 season back in her old haunts on charter to Swansea Cork Ferries whose service Strintzis later owned between 1993 and 1998, but seems set to see out the final stage of her career among the quieter seas of the Ionian islands.

In contrast, the compact *Kefalonia* originated in Japan as the *Venus* of the Higashi Nippon fleet before being elegantly rebuilt in Greece in 1995 to operate on the other Strintzis domestic service in the Adriatic, the twice daily circuit from Patras to the island whose name she carries and to the nearby island of Ithaca. She has proved a highly satisfactory

member of the fleet with a reserve of power which makes her one of the most punctual ships engaged on island services, a quality which has built a loyal following among the island dwellers.

The only vessel in the Strintzis fleet built in Australia, the *Ionian Bridge* served from 1976 until 1996 as the freight ro-ro *Bass Trader* operating between Melbourne and Tasmania. Her subsequent conversion to an extremely boxy vessel in Perama has done little for a ship whose profile was never graceful, but her large vehicle decks and powerful MAN engines have considerably improved the reliability of Strintzis service between Brindisi, Corfu and Igoumenitsa which she took over in 1997 from the *Ionian Sun*. She offers camping on board facilities, otherwise offered on the routes from Brindisi only by Med Link Lines. The timing of her route, leaving Igoumenitsa before midnight and Corfu at one in the morning to arrive in Brindisi at seven o'clock makes this way of travelling popular with impecunious campers. Equally her large vehicle decks provide scope for good freight loadings, which have been relatively uncommon on the shorter Adriatic routes in the past.

The very similar sister ships *Ionian Galaxy* and *Ionian Island* built in Japan in 1972 and 1973 were rebuilt with unusual elegance in Greece in 1987 and 1989 respectively. Both offer comfortable if now somewhat dated accommodation. The introduction of increasingly demanding safety standards, competition from newer tonnage and (not least) the availability of an alternative market saw the *Ionian Galaxy* spending much of 1998 on charter to the Libyan government operating a primarily freight route between Valetta and Tripoli as part of an attempt to circumvent United

Above: *The **Superfast I** sails for Italy.*

Below: *The **Superfast IV** at speed in the Adriatic.*

Nations sanctions against Libya. However the restoration of more normal trading conditions with Libya in early 1999 and a desire to improve the frequency, if not the speed, of Strintzis' longer services in 1999 have seen her rejoin her sister ship *Ionian Island* which continued in Adriatic service in 1998 and the pair are likely to remain in service until the introduction of the newbuildings in the new century.

Introduced to the Patras to Venice route in 1998, the *Ionian Victory* is another heavily rebuilt former Japanese vessel, built in 1974 as the *Sunflower Sapporo* she has assumed a complicated roster alternating between a twenty-three hour service between Patras and Ancona and the longer service to Venice. A relatively elegant Japanese ferry before rebuilding, the blue hull and enlarged passenger accommodation added since purchase by Strintzis have led to one of the more attractive of the recent conversions to operate on the Adriatic.

The newest ship currently in Strintzis' fleet is the *Superferry Hellas*, built in Japan in 1987 as the *Varuna* for the Higashi Nippon fleet from which the *Kefalonia* also emerged. Although built principally as a freight ferry with very limited cabin accommodation, she was an unusually

elegant ship of her type before rebuilding and was heavily remodelled at Perama before entering service in early 1999. She principally operates the 23-hour service to Ancona from Patras and is helping to keep Strintzis in the front rank of Adriatic operators until the new vessels arrive and take up more active competition with Minoan and Superfast.

The newbuilding to replace the *Eptanisos* in the year 2000, *Superferry Ithaki* was the subject of some characteristically hard bargaining by Strintzis, involving the struggling Hellenic shipyard in Elefsis. The Greek government wanted to see a ferry built in Greece for the first time in over twenty years but was frustrated by their unsuccessful struggle to meet the criteria required to bring the Greek drachma into the Euro and a South Korean shipyard desperate to break into the European ferry market. Ultimately this led to the placing of the order with Daewoo in South Korea at a price which European yards could not hope to meet on ordinary commercial terms. She is likely to offer a measured improvement in a capacity and service over her elderly predecessor, without attempting to introduce the revolution which has taken place on Adriatic international routes. The negotiations with Hellenic Shipyards have however eventually borne fruit with the order of the first major ferry order to be placed in Greece for a generation, described in Chapter 17.

In contrast, the two newbuildings currently on order from Van der Giessen's yard at Krimpen-aan-de-Ijssel in the suburbs of Rotterdam, which the company has announced will be named *Superferry Europe I* and *II*, promise a change in the style of Strintzis' Adriatic services. Designed to operate to a 28-knot speed (in contrast to the 23 knots of the *Superfast Hellas*) they are due for delivery in April and June 2000. Although seen by their builders as ro-pax vessels, they will in fact combine all of the features of the Greek ferry of the late 1990s with extensive freight and camping on board facilities as well as comfortable passenger accommodation. The initial publicity suggested that the first ship will operate between Patras and Brindisi on an eight-hour schedule while her sister will run from Patras to Ancona on an eighteen-hour schedule. Whether the Brindisi route will support such an expensive new vessel or if the advantages or a daily fast service to Ancona using both ships will prove more attractive will have to await their delivery.

There is as yet no indication that Strintzis intend to emulate in the Adriatic the interest in fast craft that they have recently displayed in the Aegean, but this innovative company is unlikely to fail to respond should competition from other fast ferry operators rise above the intermittent nuisance which previous operations by former Russian craft on the domestic routes have provided in past years.

Superfast Ferries

The instruments of revolutionary change on the Adriatic, loved and loathed in equal measure, the Ferrari-red ships of Superfast have brought a new concept in transport to the Greek ferry scene and revolutionised the way that it has been perceived by both the Athens stock market and its customers. In the process they have driven off the Adriatic many previously well established ships and have repeatedly threatened to expand their empire into the Aegean and the very heart of Greek domestic operations.

Superfast Ferries, the brilliant marketing name of the publicly quoted Attica Enterprises S.A., remains under the direction of Perikles Panagopoulos and his son Alexander who made their first fortune by developing and then selling Royal Cruise Lines to Kloster. After further success in the ownership of bulk carriers they achieved a reverse take over of Attica Enterprises in 1992 – a diverse industrial group with an established listing on the Athens Stock Exchange. The activities of the group were rapidly refocused on shipping, although the company is still defiantly listed as an 'industrial' rather than a shipping company. By ordering their first pair of ships from Schichau Seebeckwerft shortly before Minoan Lines placed their order for the *Aretousa*, the company began the process of storming the portals of the previously intensely traditional (if highly competitive) world of Adriatic ferry shipping. The order for the second pair from Kvaerner Masa yards in Finland and then the subsequent order for six more from HDW in Kiel have taken the breath from all but their most determined opponents. While only a fool would suggest that this company will not be expanding in the Adriatic still further, expansion may come from an opening of competition in other domestic markets to Crete and Rhodes and possibly to other island groups. The company has continued to maintain a canny silence on its plans in contrast to the trumpeting of rival companies and in the process has been able to repeatedly seize the initiative from them. In 1998, only four years after the start of operations, the four ships of the company took 22.7% of all passengers and 25.4% of commercial vehicles between Greece and Italy leaving the balance to 35 competing vessels.

The first pair of ships were advertised to offer a 27.9 knot maximum speed at the time of their introduction on the Patras to Ancona non-stop service in 1995 and provide an impressive 1,850 lane metres of freight space, while offering passenger accommodation for almost 1,400 of whom 626 are berthed. In their first season the pair carried over 220,000 passengers and 50,000 cars as well as a substantial proportion of the available freight traffic and, while this undoubtedly contributed to the growth of the market, it was no surprise when a number of the companies operating older tonnage responded to the competition by withdrawing their vessels to lay up at Elefsis and have subsequently left the market.

Admirably quick on their feet in the battle for dominance in the Adriatic, the perceived wisdom that Superfast placed the order for their second pair of ships in response to Minoan's announcement of their orders for the *Ikarus* and *Pasiphae* ignores the forward planning of the business which had long intended to enter the trade from Bari in addition to operating to Ancona. The Finnish sisters are a lineal development of the earlier pair, the change in shipyard being due as much to the collapse of the German yard as any indication of dissatisfaction with the earlier ships. Entering service in April and June 1998, numbers III and IV have exploited their enlarged capacity in taking over the Ancona route to provide daily sailings in the evening at seven from Italy and eight o'clock from Patras with arrival 19½ hours later, freeing the slightly older pair to a daily departure at six o'clock in the evening from Patras (midnight from Igoumenitsa) to achieve an arrival in Bari at eight thirty the next morning. Even the modest facilities of this Italian port provide a generous lay over before the vessel departs for Greece at eight in the evening, reaching Igoumenitsa at six and Patras at thirty minutes after noon the next day. The newer pair provide a slightly faster service speed of 28.5 knots and have contributed to a further enlargement of Superfast's share of this expanding market. By sensibly omitting an Igoumenitsa call from the longer service the company has avoided Minoan's difficulties with delay to Patras arrivals while carrying much traffic from northern Greece on the Bari route.

which is desperately short of fast ferries with good passenger and freight capacity it is hard to imagine that Superfast will fail to capitalise on their assets even if conditions do not allow an early introduction into Greek domestic service. Although their deployment remains a matter for conjecture at the time that this book closed for press the possible doubling of frequency on the current routes and the introduction of a Venice service would leave their rivals severely exposed and put Superfast into an unassailable lead in the Adriatic.

Turkish Maritime Lines

The state-owned long distance Turkish ferry company has extensive operations around both the Mediterranean and Black Sea coasts of its native land but qualifies for inclusion here due to its regular operations of three modern car ferries between Brindisi and Çesme. Between them offering six departures weekly (mainly on Wednesdays and Saturdays), the *Ankara*, *Iskenderun* and *Samsum* operate through the Corinth Canal. Their predictably mainly Turkish passenger complement has the opportunity of seeing this remarkable sight some twelve hours after leaving the Italian port.

Vefa Lines

The first operator to attempt a full ferry service between the Greek mainland and Albania, Vefa Lines experienced a predictable series of fluctuations in fortune as the fragile economy and political uncertainty of dealings with Albania have in turns improved and deteriorated. Operating between Patras and Durres it offers a by-pass around the execrable roads and criminal gangs of the area around the southern port of Sarande in the south of Albania but lacks an obvious market. While there are a quarter of a million Albanians legally working in Greece, and very many more illegal immigrants, they are the poorest section of the population with little scope for anything beyond migrant passenger traffic. Albania offers little obvious freight traffic for such a service, although much foreign aid is taken from Italy by Adriatica Ferries. The vessel used has been the *Aulona*, originally built in 1965 as the Lion Ferry *Gustav Vasa* but with later service in the Mediterranean for much longer than she managed in the Baltic with a variety of secondary operators.

While the other operators in the Adriatic all offer services at varying times of day and do not operate at all on some days – a failing even shared by the otherwise admirable Minoan Lines – Superfast operate to regular departure times daily throughout the year and achieve their scheduled arrivals with clockwork precision in marked contrast to most of their rivals. Within their exhausting timetables time is found to maintain the ships in immaculate condition, the external condition in particular surpasses that achieved by any other ferry operator and most cruise lines.

The subsequent vessels due for delivery from Kiel in 2000 and 2001 are unlikely to represent a major increase in speed or capacity compared to the existing members of the fleet. They do however represent a potent threat to other parts of the Greek ferry business, the target of which will not be announced until nearer to their delivery point. In a market

Above: *At Patras in the summer of 1994, A.K. Ventouris' **Agia Methodia** was subsequently chartered to Eurolink to operate between Sheerness and Vlissingen. She has since been acquired by NEL for further service in the Aegean.*

Above: *Ventouris Ferries' **Saturnus** displaying her insect-like stern ramps as she arrives in Patras.*

Typical of her period, she provides basic accommodation for 1,100 passengers and 432 lane metres of freight.

A. K. Ventouris

In the early 1990s it seemed that nothing could stop the various companies controlled by the four Ventouris brothers from steadily expanding their tentacles across the Greek ferry business. Subsequent scandal and bad luck, combined with the unforeseen explosion of new capital investment in Superfast Ferries, Minoan Lines, ANEK and Strintzis have all contributed to these companies losing their way as the 1990s have come towards their end. The interesting fleet of A.K. Ventouris (controlled by Apostolos K. Ventouris), did not operate in 1998 and the vessels remained laid-up at Elefsis or were chartered out, although in 1999 the company tentatively re-entered the increasingly competitive and somewhat oversupplied market.

The oldest vessel in the fleet, the *Igoumenitsa Express* was built as the *Cerdic Ferry* and is the third member of the Atlantic Steam Navigation Company's Transport Ferry Service fleet to operate on the Adriatic in recent years (see also

Agoudimos' *Kapetan Alexandros A* and Med Link Lines' *Afrodite II* described above). In 1999 she was on charter for service in the Black Sea as the *Clydesdale*. The fleet also included the *Agios Vassilios*, one of the earliest car ferries operating on the Baltic between Germany and Finland as the *Hansa Express* from 1962 until 1966 and subsequently for the Polish shipping company until sale to Fragline as the *Eolos* between 1981 and 1994. She has since been chartered out for service in the Black Sea as the *Orestes*. Also in the fleet was the *Arion*, one of the more remarkable vessels in the Greek ferry services in the early 1990s having spent her earlier years with Atlantic Container Line as an ocean going ro-ro vessel. She has also been chartered out following the suspension of the service. They have also recently operated the *Anna V* (now the *Jupiter* of Anatolia Ferries reviewed above) but perhaps are best known in northern Europe for having supplied to Eurolink Ferries the chartered tonnage which replaced the luxurious Olau Line ships on the Sheerness to Vlissingen service in 1994. These vessels *Euromagique* and *Euromantique* had previously spent a short period in the Adriatic on routes which suited them rather

Above: *Heavily rebuilt after service as North Sea Ferries' **Norwind**, the **Grecia Express** of Ventouris Ferries approaches Patras in 1990. She continued in operation with the company until 1994.*

Above: *Virtually unique in the Greek ferry fleet for her use of a bow door, Ventouris Ferries' **Polaris** at Patras. She has since been chartered for service in the Baltic.*

better than the chilly passage of the southern North Sea on which much of the reputation of their owners as well as their charterers was lost.

The company operated independent services from Brindisi to Igoumenitsa and to Patras, the latter requiring a lengthy non-stop passage of sixteen and a half hours despite comparatively limited on board facilities. It was not entirely surprising that the company found it hard to maintain competition with rival companies operating well-equipped modern ships to Ancona, twice the distance in an only slightly greater passage time. The re-emergence of the company with a largely freight service between Bari and Patras has required a considerable reduction in the fares and an

Above: An improbably hideous product of the Robb Caledon yard in Dundee, Vergina Ferries' *Valentino* was originally built for service in the Caribbean and has been radically altered to the detriment of her appearance since coming to the Mediterranean.

acceptance of the nature of the traffic that will be attracted by doing so. The vessel used is the unlovely *Euromagique* whose open upper deck provides air to animals on lorries in transit to Greece but whose limited passenger accommodation has made no more favourable impression than she managed when crossing the North Sea where her peculiar name was bestowed on her.

Ventouris Ferries

The largest of the companies set up by the prolific Ventouris brothers and the dominant company on Adriatic routes in the late 1980s and early 1990s, Ventouris Ferries has become a victim of the same difficulties that have faced the other family companies. Under the control of George Ventouris, it has operated a number of vessels with interesting histories, some of which remain in service and it continues to provide a good network of services from the port of Bari to Corfu and Igoumenitsa.

The company's operations began in 1984 with the purchase of the Belgian RMT's elegant car ferry *Princesse Astrid* which operated for the company until the end of the 1998 season as the *Bari Express*, although she was transferred to operate in the Aegean after the 1988 season having rapidly become too small for the trade. Her first running mate was the former British Rail *St. George*, which operated as *Patra Express* until being sold for cruising in Florida in 1989. They were then joined by the former North Sea Ferries *Norwind* in 1988 which was renamed the *Grecia Express*. Unattractively rebuilt and unusually unbecoming in the company's white livery, she lasted until 1994 when she was sunk by an explosion in still unexplained circumstances whilst laid-up at Perama. Criminal charges were suggested at one stage against those involved with the sinking, but the company survived the scandal and has continued to operate until the present despite the increasing influence of rival operators with capital raised on the Athens stock market and the plethora of new and faster ships they have introduced.

Longest serving of the current fleet is the *Athens Express*, built in 1969 she is another of the Adriatic vessels to have been built in Australia as the *Brisbane Trader* for service with the Australian National Line. Endowed with

curiously poky twin funnel and limited superstructure for service on the east coast of Australia, she joined the Ventouris Ferries fleet in 1986 following rebuilding in Greece which enlarged her passenger accommodation but did little to make her an object of beauty and failed to change her horrid little funnels. In 1998 and 1999 she has been the principal vessel on the Bari to Igoumenitsa service.

In the mid-1970s DFDS replaced their first generation of ro-ro freighters on the North Sea with a pair of vessels that were perhaps built two decades too soon. Among the last products of the Helsingør shipyard, the two large freighters *Dana Futura* and *Dana Gloria* were built with the remarkably fast speed for freighters of their time of 22.5 knots and greatly enhanced the freight service between Esbjerg in Denmark and Harwich / Felixstowe in the UK. They were, however, too sophisticated and too expensive for the then market conditions and periods of lay up in the early 1980s punctuated with short term charters preceded sale out of the fleet ten years before the return of this size and speed of freighter to the DFDS fleet. This was however, to the good fortune of Ventouris who first acquired the *Dana Hafnia* (ex *Dana Gloria*) in 1989 after three years service between Travemunde and Gedser in Denmark as the *Gedser Link* during which she was converted and her passenger capacity enlarged from twelve to 600. After further rebuilding in Greece during 1989/90 she entered Adriatic service as the *Venus* presenting a somewhat bitty appearance, but uncompromisingly the largest freight carrier and fastest vessel in the Bari to Patras service of her day. She was chartered in early 1999 by Swansea-Cork Ferries to open their service from Cork to Saint Malo.

Her sister ship stayed with DFDS until chartered in late 1988 by Nordo-Link for service between Malmo in Sweden and Travemunde, in which port she continued to encounter her sister. She had been lengthened while in DFDS service by some 32 metres and was further rebuilt at Landskrona before spending five years in the southern Baltic as the *Skåne Link*. She was then sold in the winter of 1993/4 to join her sister in the Ventouris fleet as the *Polaris*. Some modest additions were made to her superstructure which by now had a very disjointed appearance, but it was in her internal layout that

Above: *Extensively rebuilt following purchase by the Zakynthos Shipping Company, the **Zakynthos I** arrives in Kilini in the summer of 1998 and prepares to drop her anchors prior to berthing.*

she differed most markedly with loading ramps organised most effectively for loading and discharge over the bow. As a result, in complete contrast to almost every other ship described in this book, she continued to load over the bow where the ships that she has shared port with have used their opening bows (if at all) purely as a vent for exhaust fumes. However, despite her speed and enormous carry capacity for lorries, she fell victim to the intense competition in the Adriatic in 1998 and has subsequently been chartered back to her former owners Nordo-Link to resume service on their thriving service from Malmo. Initially the charter is for one year but it must be questionable whether she will in fact sail again for Ventouris Ferries.

The other two ships in Ventouris Ferries' Adriatic fleet, the *Vega* and *Saturnus* have operated on the Brindisi to Igoumenitsa service in recent years, alternating in 1999 to serve Bari as their Italian port. Generally similar in appearance, although the funnels of the *Saturnus* are much lower than those of her running mate, both were built at Trondheim in Norway within a year of one another. Early service in Scandinavia, interrupted in the case of the *Vega* by a season with Brittany Ferries as their first *Prince de Bretagne* and with *Saturnus* by a spell on charter to Townsend Thoresen in 1974 on the Dover-Zeebrugge route when she was named the *Scandinavia*, has been followed by lengthening and subsequent sale for Mediterranean operation in 1987 and 1986 respectively. After operating as the *Atlas III* and *Atlas IV* they entered the Ventouris Ferries fleet at its period of greatest expansion in 1990 and 1991. Lengthening and rebuilding of their superstructure after sale to Greece have resolved earlier problems of lack of capacity and both now possess enormous folding ramps to their upper vehicle decks, giving the impression of sinister insects as they are

unfolded prior to berthing.

Despite the problems that have afflicted other companies owned by members of the Ventouris family (see Chapter 13), the Ventouris Ferries operation in the Adriatic provides real competition to the larger and faster, but significantly more expensive, lines using more recent and capital intensive tonnage.

Vergina Ferries

Having for a while traded as Mediterranean Lines, this company continues to operate two of the most spectacularly ugly ships in service in the Adriatic on a route between Patras and Brindisi (with some diversions via Igoumenitsa) primarily to serve the commercial vehicle market, but also carrying many holiday vehicles during the summer. The company thrives in the current market by dogged determination in a highly competitive environment. The style of both ships (radically different from one another and an ill-matched pair for capacity) deserves the same violent retribution on their marine architects as most Greek urban architecture of the post war era should bring on the heads of their counterparts ashore.

The two ships can be briefly described; the *Brindisi* is an example of the large and spacious ferry ships built in Japan in the late sixties at a time when northern European ferry lines were specifying tentatively to provide space for a dozen lorries in their primarily passenger vessels. Her modest sixteen-knot speed and unsophisticated passenger accommodation do little to attract the loyalty of the passengers who sail with her, but her energetic marketing in Italy and the ability to camp on board both ships (perhaps as an answer to the catering) sees good passenger loads to balance the year round freight traffic. Her running mate

Above: *There was little to give away the origin of the Tyne-built Ellerman cargo liner* **City of York** *of 1953 following her extraordinary conversion to a car ferry for Karageorgis Lines as their* **Mediterranean Sky**. *She is seen being manoeuvred in Patras by the local tug Starlet in the summer of 1990 when near to the end of her long service with the company.*

Valentino is a somewhat improbable product of the former Robb Caledon shipyard in Leith, Scotland. Extensively and unattractively rebuilt on several occasions during her life, she represents a visual affront to the ports that she serves and it is to be hoped that Europe's under-employed ship breaking industry will soon be allowed the chance to remove this blot on the Adriatic seascape.

Zakynthos

Ferry services to the southern most of the Ionian Islands are provided by a consortium of companies operating from Kilini on the western coast of the Peloponnese. Until recently the collection of vessels included the remarkable survival of the one time British Railways (Southern Region) Channel Islands freighter *Moose*, but now the service is provided by a consortium containing Miras Ferries, Tyrogalas Lines and the Zakynthos Shipping Company.

Oldest of the current vessels, having been built as a conventional coaster in 1972 in Le Havre, the *Dimitrios Miras* has been rebuilt and renamed on several occasions before assuming her current rather basic outline in 1988. She has tended to operate the freight and supply sailings on the route although the financial problems of her parent group, considered in Chapter 17, mean that her long-term future is in doubt. The two vessels in the Tyrogalas fleet, the *Ionis* and *Proteus* were both built in Greece and have an elegance which is lacking in the other ships in the consortium. Whilst small and with limited vehicle capacity, they ideally suit the ninety-minute crossing with its strongly seasonal passenger service. The fourth member of the combined fleet, the *Zakynthos I* was originally built in Germany for service as the *Ville De Corte* before massive and hideous rebuilding in Greece in 1989 which lengthened her and enlarged her superstructure, added short side blisters and created a blot on the seascape of the southern Adriatic. Her interior is considerably more elegant that the outside of the ship would suggest.

Other Operators

The nature of traffic on the Adriatic ferry services encourages the regular introduction of new vessels by hitherto unknown operators and, almost equally quickly, their disappearance. A saunter through the shipping offices that line the harbour fronts in Patras and Igoumenitsa will unfailingly turn up publicity for other companies not mentioned in this book, some of which may indeed take up regular and successful service while others will seem to do little other than accept bookings without having taken the preliminary step of securing a vessel, crew or berthing arrangements and are not heard of again. Unsettling for the traveller who is eager to pay an early deposit to a company which has not yet begun operations, it is nonetheless among these entrepreneurial operations that some of the most interesting ferries are to be found, many having a long history and a string of former names.

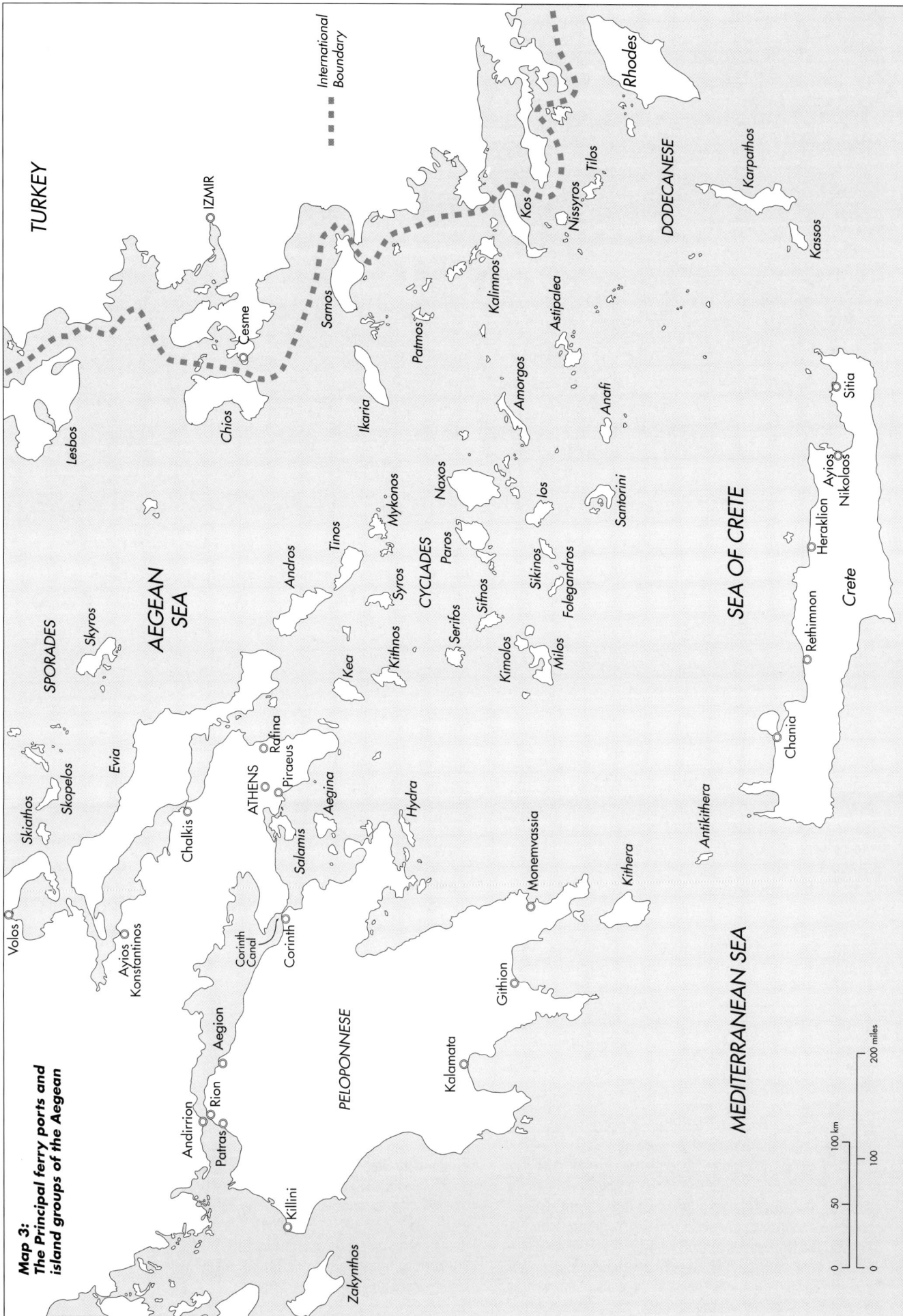

Map 3:
The Principal ferry ports and island groups of the Aegean

TURKEY

IZMIR

Cesme

International
Boundary

Rhodes

DODECANESE

Karpathos

Kassos

Tilos

Nissyros

Kos

Kalimnos

Astipalea

Patmos

Amorgos

Anafi

Ikaria

Samos

Chios

Lesbos

Naxos

Mykonos

Ios

Santorini

Tinos

Paros

Andros

Syros

Sikinos

CYCLADES

Serifos

Sifnos

Folegandros

Kea

Kithnos

Kimolos

Milos

SPORADES

Skyros

AEGEAN
SEA

SEA OF CRETE

Sitia

Ayios
Nikolaos

Heraklion

Crete

Rethimnon

Chania

Skiathos

Skopelos

Evia

Volos

Ayios
Konstantinos

Chalkis

Rafina

ATHENS

Piraeus

Aegina

Salamis

Hydra

Corinth
Canal

Corinth

Aegion

Rion

Andirrion

Patras

Killini

Zakynthos

PELOPONNESE

Kalamata

Githion

Monemvassia

Kithera

Antikithera

MEDITERRANEAN SEA

200 miles

100 km

100

50

0

0

Ferry Services of Eastern Greece

Chapter 11

Landscape and Seascape

In complete contrast to the ferry services in the Adriatic which are overwhelmingly focused around four mainland ports and are of a predominantly international character, the services in the Aegean are centred on Piraeus – the Port of Athens. They are almost entirely domestic in their character and range of destinations and the companies that serve them are far more diverse. The effect of the cabotage system is that all vessels used on domestic services are registered in Greece, owned by Greek ship owners and crewed by Greek seafarers.

In the centre of the Aegean are the Cyclades, a group of thirty islands forming a rough circle around the mythological centre of the world at the island of Delos. The Sporades are four principal islands and numerous smaller islets off the coast of mainland Greece, roughly mid-way between Athens and Thessalonika. Generally the most fertile of the Aegean Islands, Chios and Lesbos lie off the coast of Turkey while, south of them, the Dodecanese are a group of twelve islands at the south-eastern corner of the Aegean Sea having a markedly separate history from the other islands and which were only officially united to Greece in 1947. The largest of the Greek islands, Crete lies below the latitude of the north coast of Tunisia and again has a separate history derived both from its distinct history and severe geography. Other islands, both great and small, scattered throughout the Aegean attract business from the ferry companies and contribute to a comprehensive network which has developed to provide regular services to all of the inhabited islands.

Ferry services in the Aegean have grown in an apparently haphazard way, government interference has rarely taken the form of subsidies to the operators being achieved by control of the licensing of services while slow change to the now universal car ferry (whether or not the island served has any significant road network) has arisen from local demand and the enterprise of the shipping companies that have served it. Few of the vessels used carried significant quantities of vehicular traffic until the early 1970s, traditionally they were relatively small locally-built ships or were acquired second-hand from the shipping companies of northern Europe.

As the first generation of car ferries from northern Europe came to the second-hand market in the 1970s the pattern of operations has changed to centre on vehicle traffic but the comparatively small harbours in most island ports ensured that services have remained in the hands of relatively compact ferries withdrawn from northern Europe. As that supply has dwindled it has not until now been matched by alternatives from elsewhere. At the close of the 1990s a perceived need to introduce new tonnage, encouraged by

Below: *Formerly the Holyhead to Dun Laoghaire stalwart* **St Columba** *and later the* **Stena Hibernia**, *Agapitos Express Ferries'* **Express Aphrodite** *speeds down the Aegean in 1997.*

Above: *Originally Sealink's* **Senlac***, Agapitos Express's* **Express Apollon** *had a lengthy spell in the Ventouris Sea Lines fleet as the* **Apollo Express I***. She is seen during that part of her career off Salamis in 1994.*

unsophisticated political pressure from Athens, has seen the first significant orders in a generation. At the same time the assortment of companies that have operated in these trades in aggressive competition with each other, but have managed to balance the relatively modest initial outlay required with the equally modest fares that been permitted by the government, have faced financial problems in reconciling the need for the purchase of new tonnage with reducing demand. The effect has been consolidation of operations, both by direct acquisition and by the taking of cross shareholdings between medium-sized players to help to defend their share holdings against predatory attack from larger groups.

International services have a relatively small part to play in the Aegean, there are a present no international services from Piraeus to Turkey and the range of destinations available is effectively confined to the two companies competing on the route via Rhodes to Cyprus and Israel. The summer cruise ferry operation via Cyprus to Egypt (described in Chapter 18) is all that remains of the network of ferry services that until recently connected Greece with the Middle East.

The Aegean also sees a number of services provided by landing craft ferries of a similar type to those in the Adriatic. The pattern of services in the Aegean is completed by a network of fast ferry services, mainly provided by hydrofoils built in the former Soviet Union. Around seventy of these craft operate around the Aegean islands and provide a quicker (albeit noisy and uncomfortable) method of travel. Their service speed is little more than fifty percent more than that managed by elderly conventional tonnage, but they are able to provide a frequency and convenience of timetable which continues to attract a profitable segment of traffic during the summer.

Although the sea services of the Aegean may appear to be frequent and wide ranging, they are in fact grouped among carefully defined groups of islands and opportunities to interchange between those routes without having to return to Piraeus are limited. Although traditionally the island of Syros in the Cyclades has been a meeting point of Aegean ferries, the more recent growth in popularity of Paros and Mykonos have persuaded some companies to substitute calls at those islands en route to their principal destinations but communication between islands which are not of the same group remains difficult.

Although generally perceived as a calm and warm sea, the word Aegean is derived from a word which describes the sudden gales which affect it. The north-easterly wind known as Meltimi is particularly prevalent in the holiday season of high summer, and whilst cooling and clearing the air of Athens, will make many sea passages uncomfortably lively, an experience emphasised by the apparently universal trait of Greek passengers as bad sailors.

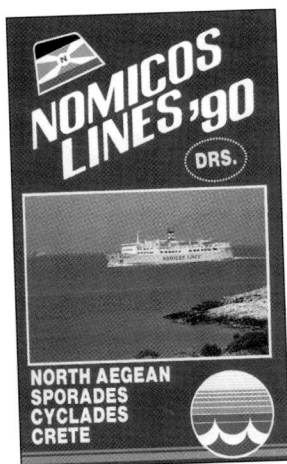

International Services

*D*espite Greece's strategic situation at the south-eastern corner of Europe, her traditionally hostile relations with Turkey and the uncertain political stability of many parts of the Middle East have led to a very limited sea trade between Greece and her eastern neighbours. As a result the number of truly long-haul operation is negligible and those that do operate are obliged to advertise themselves as the equivalent of cruise services in order to scratch a living sailing on what are in fact some of the most delightful sea routes in the Mediterranean.

During the last twenty years many companies have struggled without success to operate regular and profitable ferry services in the eastern Mediterranean. By 1999 only two remained in operation and of these Poseidon Lines had indicated that the profitability was not high enough to justify continuance in the trade. It is apparent that these operations will remain quite literally a backwater to the Greek ferry scene.

The oldest vessel in the service is now the *Nissos Kypros*, the sole vessel of Salamis Lines. She is also one of the most beautiful of European ferries having been built in 1958 for Swedish Railways as their *Trelleborg* to operate on their route from Trelleborg to Sassnitz in East Germany. The traditional straight lines of a train ferry were elegantly concealed by her designers at the long-experienced Helsingør shipyard. She was replaced in the Baltic by the delivery of new tonnage in 1977 and began her long service in Greek waters. After a further long period running to Mytilene with NEL (see Chapter 17) she came to her current owners in 1993.

Operating a weekly service, she leaves Piraeus on Thursday evenings and takes eighteen hours to reach Rhodes. Continuing to Limassol in Cyprus where she spends Saturdays, she sails at six in the evening for Haifa in Israel, which is reached at seven o'clock on Sunday morning. After a thirteen-hour layover, she returns to the same ports, reaching Piraeus at seven on Wednesday morning, giving 37 hours in port before resuming her cycle the next week. Although the long periods in port are marketed as part of the cruise element of her service, in reality the timings required by the route make a more intensive employment of the vessel impractical. The only competition she has faced in recent times has come from Poseidon Lines who have operated who have operated both the *Sea Serenade* and the *Sea Symphony* on similar timings, combining to provide a twice weekly service with little style but reasonable popularity with student travellers. It will remain to be seen whether these services will continue now that Poseidon Lines appear to have persuaded themselves of the better returns to be made from Adriatic Services and have left only the *Sea Harmony* to continue with weekly sailings leaving Piraeus on Mondays.

Small and constantly changing vessels operate between a number of the eastern islands and the Turkish mainland. The nature of the services is highly seasonal and they are more usually marketed as day excursions than proper ferry services.

Below: *The **Nissos Kypros** of Salamis Lines is seen at her berth at Piraeus after completing her long crossing from Haifa in Israel in 1995.*

Mainland to Island Services

The complex network of ferry services in the Aegean can be conveniently reviewed in a figure of eight arrangement, starting in the northern Aegean and having its centre at Paros in the Cyclades. Reference should be made to Map 3 on page 56 for a clearer picture of the locations described in the following pages.

Northern Aegean Islands

835 kilometres by road from Athens, Alexandroupolis is the last Greek city before the Turkish border and the port from which the most distant of the island links operate, to Samothrace. An ugly locally-built vessel operated by Arsinoi Lines makes the 34-kilometre crossing in two and a half hours. The most northerly of the Eastern Sporades, Samothrace is largely ignored by visitors although its detached location and the violent seas that surround it belie a beautiful island.

The closest island to Samothrace, Thassos is the most northerly island in Greece – mountainous, green and beautiful. It has achieved unexpected popularity as a package tour destination and lies only ten kilometres from the mainland. Reached by a regular service of landing craft from Kavala and a shorter thirty-minute crossing from the closest mainland town of Keramoti, it enjoys frequent services from the mainland on which some variety to the landing craft of Thassos A.N.E. is provided by the hydrofoil *Thassean Dolphin*.

The other principal Northern Aegean Island, Limnos is served by a network of larger ferries. NEL (the Maritime Company of Lesbos) provide visits by four of their vessels – *Alcaeos*, *Mytilene*, *Sappho* and the large *Theofilos* at irregular intervals and somewhat inconvenient times during the week. In addition, GA Lines provide a weekly visit with their *Romilda* (originally Townsend's *Free Enterprise VIII*) on a complicated service between Rhodes and Alexandroupolis.

The Sporades

South-west of Limnos and principally served from the mainland port of Volos, the islands of the Sporades are beautiful, sparkling and over-loaded by their summer visitors. In addition to visits by ferries from Thessalonika, their principal connections with the mainland and with one another are provided by the elderly and eccentric *Papadiamantis II* of Goutos Lines and an assortment of vessels from the fleet of Nomicos Lines.

The Sporades (or 'scattered') islands are Skiathos, Skopelos, Alonissos and some way to the east, Skiros – the largest of the group. They enjoy a frequent service from the Nomicos fleet and from a network of services provided by Flying Dolphins operating both from the mainland ports of Volos and Ayios Konstantinos. However, they receive

most of their visitors by direct charter flights from northern Europe, arriving at the noisy airport of Skiathos from where the holiday makers are distributed around the chain of islands by ferries and other charter vessels.

Notwithstanding the small size and comparatively advanced age of the ferries serving the island group, the connections between the islands are poor and they see little connection with other services running in the Aegean.

Evia

To the south of the Sporades and more commonly known in classical times as Euboea, Greece's second largest island enjoys a wide variety of ferry services but is largely ignored by foreign visitors. It offers a charming, if uncompromisingly Greek, exception to the pattern of small and over-touristed islands in the Aegean.

The island capital is at Chalkis – itself partly built on the mainland and linked to the island by a swing bridge. A busy commercial town, Chalkis has no ferry services of its own but provides a final resting place for numerous laid-up passenger and cargo vessels including the former Polish Atlantic liner *Stefan Batory* in addition to the one-time *Compiegne* – see Chapter 19.

At its northern point, Evia has a car ferry operated by a single landing craft running between the small town of Glifa on the mainland close to the National Road to Thessalonika and the small island slipway of Agiokampos. It can be linked with the ferry service to Arkitsa, considered below, to save a lengthy drive along this hideous motorway.

Five kilometres south of Agiokampos is the spa town and resort of Loutro Edipsos. Although the concept of the spa in northern Europe may evoke images of Harrogate and Baden-Baden, in Greece it remains a popular and unpretentious mixture of holiday and healing with a large input from the Orthodox Church. To serve the throng of visitors, there is a 45-minute frequency on the car ferry service over the North Evia Channel to the mainland port of Arkitsa immediately adjoining the National Road referred to above.

Undoubtedly the most attractive of the ferry services to Evia is that from the mainland slipway of Agia Marina to Nea Styra. Crossing the narrows of the south-end of the Evia

*Right Among the more elegant of the Greek-built ferries of the mid-1970s, Nomicos Lines **Lemnos** is seen off Paros.*

Left: *After initial service on the Aegina route, the peculiarly ugly landing craft **Miaoulis I** has now transferred to the short route from Ayia Marina to Styra on Evia.*

south-east from Evia.

Rafina has, until recently, provided a unique example in Greece of a consortium of major operators working together to provide an efficient daily service without wasteful competition. A triumvirate of Agoudimos Lines, Strintzis Lines and Ventouris Ferries have each contributed a single vessel to the pool, whilst jointly owning a fast ferry to provide a particularly efficient network of services.

This cosy arrangement came to an end in 1998, with an increase in sailings by Strintzis provided by the *Ionian Sun* (see Chapter 10) and the withdrawal of Ventouris Ferries from the route. Although initially the timetables from Rafina have seen few changes, Strintzis have acquired the shares from the other partners in the fast ferry and have moved to the same operation their similar Westamarin catamaran *Mirage* which has spent 1998 running from Piraeus to Aegina and renamed her *Sea Jet 2*. The operations of Ventouris were sold to Agapitos Express Ferries in 1999 and further changes to the services from the former members of the consortium can be expected as the capacity now provided appears to comfortably exceed any likely demand. Initially co-operation between Agapitos Express and Agoudimos Lines has continued but with no obvious co-ordination of the timetable, some sailings operating virtually in tandem with the available traffic divided between them

The former consortium faced increased competition during the second half of the 1990s from Goutos Lines, formerly occupied in short distance traffic from Rafina and Lavrion using an improbable car-carrying catamaran and an FBM tri-cat, built at Cowes on the Isle of Wight.

The services aimed at the northern Cyclades meet and connect with a number of the services from Piraeus travelling to the central and eastern islands considered below. The islands vary between the mainly agricultural Andros and disco-deafened Mykonos. Perhaps the ultimate Greek holiday destination, Mykonos throbs with activity until dawn, but its notoriety as the setting for the film *Shirley Valentine* and its reputation for promiscuity ensure not only an endless flow of hopeful tourists, but also plenty of rowdy Athenians looking for entertainment. Between Andros and Mykonos lies the spiritual centre of modern Greece, the lovely island of Tinos. Dominated by its cathedral dedicated to the Virgin Mary (the name of which, *Panagia Tinou,* was carried by two generations of ferries on the main day sailing from Piraeus), the island sees the peak of its activity around the Holy Feast of the Dormition of the Virgin, at the height of the tourist season on 15th August. To the protestant visitor from northern Europe, the procession of the miracle-working icon from the cathedral around the town on the Feast Day is a sobering insight into a religion centred on a popular spirituality which much of Europe now lacks. The other significant island of the group is Syros, the capital of the county of the Cyclades and for long a crossroads of ferry services in the eastern Mediterranean. Although this role has now passed to Paros, the main town of Ermoupolis with its two hills topped by churches, one Catholic

Channel, it passes between innumerable islets between which the white landing craft ferries weave their passage to the island resort town. Operating to a leisurely and irregular timetable, it crosses over magnificently clear water through wide bays.

Further south, two irregular routes run from Athens' second port, Rafina. They serve the twin villages of Marmari and Karystos, using the only two proper ferries (as opposed to landing craft) which serve Evia which between them provide four or five daily departures from Marmari and three or four from Karystos. Both have been operated by Goutos Lines before their seduction into the fast ferry fashions of the 1990s and have been taken up respectively by DD Ferries and Mililis Lines. Although both are utilitarian in their accommodation, the two vessels provide a lovely crossing and some of the nearest sensation of the peace of the Aegean Islands to the capital city.

Kea

For long the haunt of the former Mersey ferry *Royal Daffodil II*, a ferry runs from Lavrion near Cape Sounion at the south-eastern corner of the Greek mainland to the delightfully under-visited island of Kea. Twice daily crossings on weekdays are increased to operate five times daily at weekends since the island is a popular weekend retreat for Athenians. The 75-minute crossing of the Kea Channel passes over the wreck of the hospital ship *Britannic*, a sister ship of the *Titanic*, sunk by a mine on 21st November 1916 en route to the Dardenelles. The vessel now lies over 100 metres down but has been investigated by the same team of marine archaeologists who have brought back such uncomfortable video scenes from the wreck of her sister ship in mid-Atlantic.

Today, the route is operated by another of the small vessels in the fleet of Goutos Lines, the *Myrina Express* which is the only ferry regularly using the small port of Lavrion, anciently the site of the Athenian silver mines which contributed hugely to Athens' commercial and political greatness.

Cyclades – northern islands

Of all the island groups in Greece, those in the Cyclades are both the most diverse and also served by the greatest variety of ferry services. The Cyclades are the archetypal Greek holiday islands but also combine a thriving agricultural and fishing community with the business of supporting visitors. The northern islands of Andros, Tinos, Mykonos and Syros are principally served from Athens' second port of Rafina and lie

Above: *The former* **Comte De Nice** *of SNCM has sailed since 1983 as the* **Naias II** *on the intensive but relatively short route between Piraeus and Paros, Naxos and Mykonos.*

and one Orthodox, is a most attractive ferry port seeing regular sailings to most of the islands in the northern and central Cyclades.

Cyclades – central islands

At the centre of the circle of the Cyclades are some of the most heavily touristed and intensively served ferry destinations of the eastern Mediterranean. Immediately south of Delos and Mykonos, Paros is now the main interchange point between the various ferry services of the Aegean with occasional vessels on (at least the less direct) routes to almost all islands between Crete and Lesbos calling during the course of the week. There is also some of the most intense competition on the services from Piraeus, some four and a half hour's steaming away.

A little to the east is the large island of Naxos, a beautiful combination of white houses in its town and villages blending with citrus-clad hills and a rocky landscape. South of Naxos is the small and bustling island of Ios, the very opposite of an unspoilt Greek island.

Just as overwhelmed by tourists, but infinitely more spectacular in its setting and history, is the island of Santorini (also called Thira), fifteen kilometres to the south. Formed in 1500 BC by a volcanic eruption of the scale that the earth has seen on fortunately few occasions, the island slopes up to the lip of the

caldera over 300 metres above the lagoon beneath. Cliffs drop sharply to the sea, the bed of which is a further 400 metres below water level, while in the middle of the bay the small island of Therissa contains sulphur springs while little vegetation which is able to grow on the lava from which it has been formed. Today, the geological results and the delightfully situated town of Thira on the cliff's edge act as a magnet to vast numbers of tourists. The old port at the foot of the cliffs below the town is connected to its destination by a zigzag staircase of 587 steps (and a more recent cable car) but is now used mainly by the day cruise vessels from Crete (see Chapter 18) and other cruise ships. Ferry traffic is now concentrated in the southern port of Athinios, where up to a dozen ferries call daily in high summer.

It is on the route to these islands from Piraeus that some of the most intense competition between operators takes

Right: *Second of the post-war Belgian car ferries, the* **Artevelde** *of 1958 was sold to Agapitos Lines in 1976. She is seen off the island of Paros in 1980 as their* **Aigaion** *on her long route from Piraeus to Rhodes.*

place. Operations are dominated by vessels of Agapitos Lines and Agapitos Express Ferries running in intense competition with one another. Traditionally operating from Piraeus with departures around eight in the morning, competition has been based on speed and reliability with Agapitos' *Panagia Ekatontapyliani* the usual winner on both counts until the introduction of modern fast craft. Other services are provided by Arkadia Lines and Minoan Lines and more occasional calls are made at Paros by vessels on many of the longer services. 1999 saw the introduction of regular services from Rafina by the Strintzis catamaran *Seajet 2*.

Cyclades – western Islands

Exclusively served from Piraeus and with little connection to the other ferry services amongst the Cyclades, the western group includes some of the less frequently visited islands and some of the most interesting ferry services.

Laid out in a line virtually due south of Cape Sounion, the islands of Kythnos, Serifos, Sifnos, Milos and Kimolos (with the adjoining island to the east of Folegandros) combine most of the features which the visitor expects a Greek island to provide. Mountains rising sharply from the sea topped by white houses and churches, sparse vegetation and windmills are all features of the landscapes of these rocky outposts of Greece. Still dominated by farming and fishing businesses and, in the case of Milos mining operations, they have a scattering of ancient sites. One of the most beautiful relics of classical Greece, the Venus de Milo, was found in a field in the island of Milos in 1820 and taken to Paris where it stands in the Louvre. Attractive as the remains of ancient civilisations are in these islands, it is for the relative peace that they offer compared to the other Aegean islands that they are mainly noted.

The ferry services to the Cyclades western islands are far less intense and competitive than those in the central islands of the chain. The recent arrival of Flying Dolphins *Megadolphin* class of Italian-built hydrofoils has seen much of the short distance traffic from Athens to Kythnos, Serifos and Sifnos falling to the fast craft, but the chain of islands continues to be served by Lindos Lines, using their long-standing *Milos Express* running in competition with the last of the Ventouris Ferries' fleet in the Aegean, the *Pegasus*. Although both operators appear to lack the resources to fight off competition from a more aggressive intruder, the limited traffic that is available and the loss of profitable short-distance traffic to the hydrofoils means that these services have seemed impervious to competition from conventional vessels for many years.

Cyclades – eastern islands

The final parts of the Cyclades chain are a series of small and comparatively unpopulous islands spread out to the east of Naxos. For long served by occasional extensions of the sailings to the central islands of the Cyclades and some calls by vessels on routes to the Dodecanese, the purchase by Agapitos Express Ferries of the former Ventouris vessels *Panagia Tinou 2* and *Bari Express* has been followed by the acquisition of an operating licence for the latter to run five times weekly from Piraeus to Amorgos and Astipalea. Under the name *Express Hermes* the one-time Belgian Marine *Princesse Astrid* runs in competition with Agapitos Lines' *Naias Express* – also previously well known in British waters as the *Ailsa Princess* and later as *Earl Harold*. The majority of sailings among the island group are however provided by local ferries and catamarans necessitating a change to another ship to continue to or from the mainland.

Below: *The* **Milos Express** *at sea showing the additional superstructure added after her sale from the Sealink fleet in which she sailed as the* **Vortigern***; the fisherman in his small boat in the foreground is about to experience her considerable wash.*

Crete

Greece's largest island, some 300 kilometres south of Athens and a similar distance from the African Coast is over 250 kilometres in length and contains both some of the country's best beaches and most dramatic mountain scenery. It also has a considerable variety of ferry links to the mainland.

The connections with Thessalonika have been noted above – long routes down the length of the Aegean with several stops at island ports en route – both operate on a very similar timetable and terminate in the island capital of Heraklion which is also the destination of the principal services from Piraeus.

Undoubtedly the principal operator to the island, and a contender to that title in all of Greece, Minoan Lines has its headquarters in the main street of the town. Minoan Lines, taking their name from Europe's first advanced civilisation whose culture was based in palaces around the island of Crete, operate a pair of nearly identical sister ships built in Japan in the early 1970s on the long route from Athens which are due to be replaced in 2000/1 by a pair of fast new ships now under construction in Italy. Sailing nightly throughout the year at quarter past seven in the evening in each direction they arrive uncomfortably early, before six the next morning when disembarkation is required immediately. The new ships will introduce a revolution in the long standing timetable of the nightly sailings, balanced at summer weekends by additional daylight crossings - the tight turnarounds for which lead to cumulative delays by Sunday evenings of several hours. The new ships promise crossing times of little more than six hours and will surely offer later departures and (it is to be hoped) more convenient arrival times whilst having the capacity to

operate daily return crossings on a regular basis. The extent to which such capacity will be required will no doubt depend above all on the success that Minoan Lines have in capturing business from their rivals.

The principal competitors on the route are, as so often, ANEK whose headquarters are in the west of Crete at Chania. Currently operating a pair of hideous Japanese vessels, their normal departure times are thirty minutes ahead of Minoan with arrivals at correspondingly unearthly times, presumably with a view to ensuring that their passengers are unloaded before there is sufficient daylight for them to realise the full horror of the design of vessel they have travelled upon. Despite the external appearance, the warmth of the welcome makes a good match for the more conventional Minoan ships currently in service but they seem certain to suffer a considerable downturn in their market share when the new Minoan vessels are delivered.

ANEK are however far stronger of the two companies in the western port of Chania, the headquarters of the company and the terminal of the route on which it has long been the dominant operator. With nightly departures from Piraeus and Chania at half past eight and arrivals shortly after six in the morning the route provides a marginally more civilised method of travelling to the island, although arrival at Chania's port of Soudha can demoralise the most boisterous traveller. An essentially industrial area six kilometres outside the attractive harbour town, it saw some of the fiercest fighting in the German invasion of Crete of 1941 and was used as the principal Royal Navy anchorage during the period. One of the hauntingly beautiful Commonwealth War Graves Commissions cemeteries stands a little outside the port where many of the defenders lie at rest among flowers and greenery very different from the surrounding scenery.

Although Minoan have operated on the route in past years, in the late 1990s they have diverted their tonnage to operate on other routes in the Adriatic. It has however been agreed, as a condition of obtaining a licence to re-enter the trade in 2000, that a new vessel is to be introduced on to the service. It remains to be seen whether this will be achieved by diverting

Above: *The arrival of the* **Vitsentzos Kornaros** *at Sitia in Eastern Crete as a crowd of passengers, friends and well-wishers gather on the quay side while the stern ramp is lowered as the ship approaches.*

one of the recent newer vessels from the Adriatic (perhaps the *Aretousa*) or by taking one of the vessels currently booked for the Heraklion service and running it to the western island port. Although a superficial analysis would suggest that the Heraklion based company will rapidly become the dominant operator on this route as well, the fierce regional loyalty of the Cretans may well mean that the local company will retain a significant share in the business even with the onset of this substantial competition.

Crete's third city, Rethimnon, is midway between Heraklion and Chania and did not enjoy a ferry service of its own until 1992 when thrice-weekly sailings on a new route to Piraeus were introduced by the Rethimnaki Shipping Company, trading as Cretan Ferries. They now use a pair of mid-sized former Japanese ferries which provide a regular evening departure at seven thirty in each direction. Although widely and effectively marketed, the company has always appeared to operate with smaller loadings that its main competitors and in 1999 the company was acquired by ANEK. Whilst initially retaining is separate identity, change seems inevitable and the possible closure of the route is rumoured. The strategic wisdom of the purchase as a move to block out Minoan from the port may not suffice to justify a long term future for a service which operates at similar timings to those serving Heraklion and Chania, themselves only 150 kilometres apart.

Eastern Crete has a remote air, seeming far beyond Europe – an impression heightened by Europe's only natural forest of palm trees. As elsewhere on the island, the landscape is dominated by tall and barren mountains which look down upon the small port of Sitia, from where the Lassithi A.N.E.(LANE Lines) operate one of the most interesting ships currently sailing to the Island, the *Vitsentzos Kornaros* – originally Townsend Thoresen's *Viking Viscount* and subsequently P&O's *Pride of Winchester*. She was joined in

1999 by the Japanise built *Ierapetra*.

LANE also serve Ayios Nikolaos, one the principal tourist destinations on the island and one particularly patronised by Scandinavian visitors. They operate a long service from Piraeus via Milos in the western Cyclades to Ayios Nikolaos and Sitia which continues once weekly to Karpathos and Rhodes, to the north-east. Despite the comfort of the ships and the interesting route they follow, the company is the latest in a line of operators to have found competition with the main island services too much and during 1999 control passed to ANEK after an earlier exciting but unconsummated liaison with Minoan Lines.

Last of the links between Crete and the mainland is the subsidised service from the western port of Kastelli Kissamou. It is a route that has seen many operators try but ultimately abandon the route which runs via the isolated islands of Kythera and Antikythera before continuing along the coast of the Peloponnese to Piraeus. In the early 1990s the route was operated by Lindos Lines, occasionally with the *Milos Express* before changing hands in the middle of the decade and being operated by Miras Ferries with their *Theseus*. Her operators failed in the early summer of 1997 and the route was taken up at short notice by ANEK using the *Candia* – unfortunately omitting the dramatic landfall at Monemvassia towards the south-eastern corner of the Peloponnese. ANEK's strategic alliance with DANE in 1999 has seen the Japanese-built ship joining the services of the Rhodes-based operator and the future of the service is again in the balance as this book closed for press.

The Southern Peloponnese

To the north-west of Crete, the small port of Gytheion and the larger industrial port of Kalamata (scene of the decisive victory by the German invaders in 1941) enjoyed ferry services to Crete with the vessel from the Kastelli Kissamou service in the earlier parts of the 1990s. Although heavily subsidised, the political initiative which led to the establishment of these routes has not survived and only Gytheion currently sees ferry services using the *Maria-Pa* of Golden Ferries on a route that is now largely reduced to an island supply service for Kythera.

As recently as the late 1970s many of the coastal towns of the Peloponnese did not have direct road links to the outside and were dependent on a coastal ferry service latterly provided by Agapitos using the *Miaoulis* – one of three similar classic ferries built in Italy as war reparations. By the mid-1980s the Greek road network had spread its tentacles to all parts of the Peloponnese and the service was withdrawn.

The long journey from Piraeus through the Saronic Gulf Islands and down the east coast of the Peloponnese has been one of the most delightful sea journeys which Greece has offered and its disappearance has marked the

Above: *The **Aegina** arriving in Piraeus from her home island in 1990.*

end of a fascinating era in ferry operations in Greece. The withdrawal of ANEK from the service opens the possibility of a new operator resuming services to some to the coastal towns which, whilst accessible to vehicles, remain largely isolated. Until its withdrawal the regular visits of the ferry were major events in village life for which most of the population would turn out to inspect those arriving and make their farewells to those who were sailing away.

Saronic Gulf

The large gulf between the north-eastern side of the Peloponnese and the coast of Attica along which Athens sprawls contains more than a dozen relatively small islands, sparsely populated by year-round inhabitants but filled to bursting in summer by wealthy Athenians escaping the smog and heat of the capital for summer holiday homes to which they travel in large numbers in the evenings and at weekends.

While freight is delivered by unremarkable landing craft ferries from the mainland, there are few conventional vessels engaged in this trade, most making long day roundtrips from Piraeus. The largest company in the trade is Agapitos Express Ferries who operate the much-travelled *Express Danae* on a daily service from Piraeus calling at Aegina and then continuing to the islands of Methana, Poros, Ermioni, Hydra,

Above: *The **Saronikos** leaving Piraeus for Aegina, a landing craft which appears to aspire the status of a fully enclosed ferry and features the creative use of steel plate typical of the products of Perama.*

Spetses and finally to the mainland port of Porto Heli immediately north of Spetses. She occasionally exchanges schedules with the much smaller but more modern *Georgios 2* and *Eftychia* and the slightly bizarre *Saronikos* – a landing craft trying to be a real ferry.

It is however with the Kometa Hydrofoils, built in Russia between the 1970s and early '80s, that the Flying Dolphin operation provides a very large proportion of the passenger services in the Saronic Gulf. Tickets are not generally sold through agencies, simply at small kiosks on the quayside and result is a simple, efficient, and reliable operation charging fares between 50% and 100% above those applying to the conventional vessels. Their 34-knot speed and reliability, which is achieved by having a considerable proportion fleet kept spare to cope with both pre-planned and other maintenance, produces a relatively fast method of travel for the many Greek travellers prepared to sacrifice their hearing and sensitivity to vibration for the sake of an earlier arrival.

Aegina

Perhaps the most competitive part of the entire Greek ferry market, services to Aegina are provided by all of the Saronic Gulf operators described above, a consortium of landing craft operators, an assortment of fast motor boats and, in addition to a plethora of the Flying Dolphin craft similar vessels operated by Sea Falcon Lines, an isolated Westamarin W86 catamaran of Paraskevas Lines and what was, until the recent merger with Minoan Lines, the pride and joy of the Flying Dolphins fleet – the unusual passenger-only Austal catamaran *Flying Dolphin 2000*. All of these vessels compete together to serve an island just 25 kilometres south of Piraeus with an area of only 86 square kilometres and a resident population of no more than 12,500 – albeit boosted enormously by the summer weekenders from Athens and package tour holiday makers. With crossings taking only 35 minutes by hydrofoil or catamaran and 90 minutes by landing craft it is immensely accessible from the capital and the operators compete vigorously for the available traffic.

In 1998 Strintzis somewhat unexpectedly entered the trade with their then new catamaran *Mirage* operating from the same corner of Piraeus' Great Harbour as the Flying Dolphins. Extensive advertising throughout Athens and the surrounding area and the impressive nature of the new vessel failed to produce a significant dent in the market, due mainly to the

Mainland to Island Services

Right: *The extraordinary rock promontory above Monemvassia with the **Theseus** at the quay on a warm summer's evening in 1995.*

infrequency of a single ship operation with tickets that were not interchangeable with other lines. The vessel has now been transferred to operate from Rafina to the north Cyclades (see above).

Salamis

The nearest to Athens and among the nastiest of the Greek islands, Salamis lies at the northern end of the Saronic Gulf, in places less than one kilometre from the coast of the mainland. An industrial and dockyard island lacking any intrinsic charm, the island is served by a variety of ferries ranging between standard Russian-built hydrofoils through landing craft to motorboats with wooden hulls whose design is based on the ancient style of caique to be found throughout the Mediterranean.

The principal attraction, in many ways the only one, of a trip to the island is the passage of the Strait of Salamis where the Athenian navy defeated the invasion fleet of the Persians in 480 BC and set Greece on a road to pre-eminence in the Mediterranean. The battle took place in the strait between the island and what is now the shipyard town of Perama, but however notable the history and setting, the lamentable architecture and sprawling development of the island of Salamis put it towards the bottom of the holidaymaker's choice of destination.

Passenger vessels use the Great Harbour in Piraeus, tying up in the south-eastern corner and providing a grandstand view as they pass out through the harbour of the lay-up keys of Keratsini and the shipyards of Perama. The most frequent service is however the landing craft car ferry between Perama and Salamina.

To the north of the island is the bay of Elefsis, virtually a lagoon due to the surrounding mountains on the mainland and island and the narrow sea passages in and out.

The Dodecanese

Turning east from Athens and passing out through the Cyclades brings one to the Dodecanese. Although a literal translation would suggest that there were twelve islands in the chain, there are fourteen inhabited islands within the county as well as an enormous number of uninhabited islets. Their history during the last century has made them somewhat isolated from the remaining parts of Greece and is still reflected in customs concessions and the cultural independence that the islands enjoy. Remaining under Turkish rule long after the independence of the mainland, it was not until 1912 that they escaped the Ottoman Government when they were annexed by Italy. Although a treaty of 1920 should have passed government to Greece, it was subsequently repudiated by the Italians and the islands remained occupied by them until gradual occupation by British Forces towards the end of the Second World War and it was only on 7th March 1947 were they officially united to Greece. They continue to enjoy a duty free status similar to the Channel Islands, but without a separate government or financial system.

The capital of the chain of islands and by far the largest is Rhodes. One of the most tourist infested places in the Mediterranean, it also manages to combine considerable areas of unspoilt countryside and a thriving commercial life. It represents the principal draw for the two main ferry lines operating from Piraeus, but the distractions of the need to serve the other islands in the chain and the political interference of the Ministry of Shipping combine to disrupt what could be an efficient express service to the mainland.

The local operator has for many years been DANE (Dodecanese A.N.E.) which has sailed a mixture of former northern European and Japanese vessels in an interesting mixture of services.

The main competitor is GA Ferries, a company associated with the Agoudimos family but pursuing a distinctly different approach both to the area that it serves and the styles of ship that it employs. Although based in Piraeus, their ships have tended to be more popular with the islanders for the comfort of their accommodation and reliability of their services. The Japanese-built *Rodanthi* and *Marina* now operate on the fast service from Piraeus to Rhodes. Departing from both termini at four o'clock in the afternoon they reach their destination at quarter to eight the following morning. The regular calls at intermediate ports during the small hours accompanied by much dropping of anchors, announcements by tannoy aboard and the noise of passengers are inclined to prevent a great deal of sleep in the comfortable cabins on board these vessels, but the afternoon sail from Rhodes through the lovely south-eastern part of the Aegean when returning to Athens more than compensates for this disturbance. As usual the operating licences of these two ships require other diversions including twice-weekly trips around the eastern Cyclades to serve the remote islands of Amorgos and Astipalea – neither of which produce much in the way of traffic for these large and well operated ships.

GA Ferries' stopping service around the Dodecanese is maintained by another pair of Japanese ferries, the *Daliana* and *Milena* – both provide an effective means of transport to Patmos and the northern part of the Dodecanese with calls on most sailings at Paros and Naxos in the Cyclades as a convenient connection between the island chains (see Chapter 14). A Sunday lunch-time arrival at the volcanic island of Patmos aboard one of these vessels with the large monastery where St John the Divine wrote the Book of Revelation high above the port is a memorable experience of travel by Greek ferry.

The Dodecanese also see a remarkable service provided

Above: *Heavily rebuilt from her days as TT Lines' third **Nils Holgersson** prior to service between Australia and Tasmania as the **Abel Tasman**, NEL's **Theofilos** lies at her berth in Piraeus before departure to Mytilene.*

by the fifth vessel of GA Ferries, the *Romilda* – originally Townsend Thoresen's *Free Enterprise VIII* – calling at some of the smallest and least remunerative of the ports in the eastern Aegean, with some sailings taking her as far south as Sitia in eastern Crete before continuing through the Cyclades to Piraeus. The route enjoys some of the heaviest subsides provided by the Greek Government to maintain links to the smaller and more isolated islands and seems likely to continue with the current vessel for many years to come.

The future of services to the Dodecanese is likely to be dictated by the ability of DANE to recover from its current financial woes and the proposed introduction by GA Ferries of a fast craft capable of shortening the journey time to the capital to six hours or so.

The North-eastern Aegean

Returning north from the Dodecanese, the final section of the Aegean to be considered consists of a scattering of islands, many very close to the coast of Turkey. The political relations between the two countries since the disastrous attempt by Greece to annex portions of the mainland of Turkey in 1922, which ended in the mass deportation of those of Greek ethnic origin from Turkey matched by the similar removal of many of Turkish origin from Greece, have meant that islands only a few kilometres offshore have no contact with their Islamic neighbour, preferring to look hundreds of kilometres west to the Greek mainland for supplies and cultural inspiration. Ferry services divide into two routes, one serving the southern islands of Ikaria and Samos whilst separate services run to the more northerly islands of Chios and Lesbos.

Samos is one of the largest of the Greek islands, lying just

north of the Dodecanese chain. Unusual both for the extent of its tree cover and lack of tourists, the island is served both by GA Ferries' *Milena* and *Daliana* (noted above) and vessels from Nomicos Lines and Agapitos Lines. Nomicos operate the Japanese-built *Anemos* on a complicated route through the Cyclades serving both Ikaria and Samos. Agapitos operate their *Golden Vergina* – a sister of the *Naias II* sailing on the far busier route to the central Cyclades. Very long in the tooth and appearing to be shunned by the inhabitants of the islands she serves, she nonetheless carries substantial summer traffic on the comparatively sparse services provided to these islands.

The northern islands of the group are in contrast served by regular sailing of the admirable NEL, the Maritime Company of Lesbos. Although not particularly popular with visitors from abroad, the large islands of the north-eastern Aegean provide a pleasant rest from the more touristed parts of the country.

Although the services can be expected to change after 1999, with the introduction of NEL's fast monohull now being built by Alsthom Leroux and the introduction by Strintzis Lines of the new service recently awarded in a licensing exercise which has necessitated the construction of a new ship for the purpose, summer services to the islands in the 1990s have enjoyed considerable stability and quality – perhaps surprising in view of the effective monopoly of NEL. The fleet of five vessels operate complicated rosters bringing them during the course of most weeks onto each of the services operated by the company – the principal ones being to Piraeus and Thessalonika. It is to be hoped that the intensification of shipping services to these quieter islands will not lead to a change in their character or put at risk the splendid services provided in recent years.

Inter Island Services

One of the remarkable features of Greek ferries is the discrete way in which one set of services run completely separately from others. When standing on the cliffs of Milos in the western Cyclades ships can be seen passing regularly on their way to and from Crete while ships running from Piraeus to Paros, fifty kilometres to the east, are clearly visible. However the only ferry services actually to call at the island run to the other islands in the group on the service to Piraeus with the sole exception of twice-weekly continuations by the *Pegasus* of her sailings to Santorini. Apart from that the only connections to other island groups are made by hydrofoil operators and by small local boats operating to no published timetable. A similar pattern applies throughout the Aegean Islands and travelling between them requires careful planning and a degree of flexibility.

Timings from intermediate islands on services originating at or continuing to Piraeus are usually a matter of informed conjecture rather than watch-like precision and the availability of berths in the more comfortable classes of accommodation is far from guaranteed. The introduction of computerised ticketing was advertised to greatly assist the availability of accommodation for intermediate journeys but appears to have been omitted from the software programmes purchased by the ferry companies.

Exceptions to the general lack of inter-island connections by conventional ships are the useful services provided by Amorgos Ferries between the central and southern Cyclades based at Paros. Both are small ships of little over 1,000 tons and with decidedly limited facilities aboard, their operations are free of the predictability of the timetable required by mainland operators providing an early morning departure from and late evening return to Piraeus. Their small size and shallow draft mean that they are particularly exposed to disruption by this strong north-easterly wind which is a recurrent feature in the Aegean in summer and autumn and neither of these Greek vessels has a good reputation amongst visitors from elsewhere in Europe.

Similar services in the eastern Cyclades provided by the *Express Skopelitis*, but other inter-island runs are mainly provided by caiques – motorised wooden-hulled boats whose design is of great antiquity but details of whose operations are almost impossible to discover other than by personal enquiry at the relevant ports.

However, extensive inter-island services are provided in summer by fleets of the Russian-built hydrofoils. Although the large fleet of Flying Dolphins are mainly confined to services around the Saronic Gulf and along the eastern coast of the Peloponnese, the three large 'Megadolphin' type do provide regular services among the western and central Cyclades. However, it is the fleets of Ilio Hydrofoils and their derivatives, Dodecanese Hydrofoils and Speed Lines which provide the greatest variety of services throughout the Aegean. Their comparatively high speed and limited capacity makes it possible for them to provide intensive diagrams of services around the islands and, whatever their shortcomings to the ears and stomachs of their passengers they form a vital and now long-established part of the overall shipping scene.

Below: *An example of the Kokhilda class of hydrofoil, the* **Santorini Dolphin** *seen at speed off the island of Paros in 1997 on one of the summer only routes of Speed Lines.*

Piraeus

A name spoken in dread by many whose experience of Greece was obtained with backpacks in their youth, Piraeus is the ancient port of Athens and while in some parts a most delightful relief from the heat and pollution of the capital, to the unprepared and impecunious visitor it can offer some of the most disgusting features and avaricious tradesmen to be found in the entire country.

As a shipping centre, Piraeus is without peer in the Mediterranean and perhaps in the whole of Europe. Virtually all Greek businesses connected with shipping – and those from elsewhere seeking a presence in Greek shipping business – have their offices along the Akti Miaouli stretching around the southern and eastern sides of the Great Harbour. The main residential area of the town stretches out along a peninsula surrounded by walls originally constructed in the fifth century BC to the orders of Themistokles and still apparent for almost the whole of their circuit. The eastern side of the peninsula provides some of the most exclusive residential districts of Athens and is the home of the yacht harbour of Zea, at the seaward end of which is the main terminal of the Flying Dolphins operation. To the west of Piraeus ugly suburbs give way to the shipyards of Perama, continuing around the eastern side of the strait of Salamis into the bay of Elefsis where strings of vessels are chained side by side awaiting a return to service

sized dry docks. Within the harbour are fourteen distinct areas from which ferry services regularly depart (see Map 5). Although the allocation of berths is far from absolute, the quays used by the longer distance services to the north-eastern Aegean, Crete and the Dodecanese are rarely interfered with by other operators, those vessels serving the Cyclades are more promiscuous in the quays that they use. Although there are no fixed installations ashore other than mooring bollards, in the period leading up to the departure of a vessel it will be surrounded by representatives of the owners (selling tickets apparently free from the computerised system), the port police and the sellers of bread and nuts to embarking passengers.

Above: *Not an easy port for the beginner. The signs on Piraeus central ticket block in the early 1990s.*

Left: *Evening at Piraeus with Minoan Lines'* **King Minos** *arriving from Heraklion, a caique arriving from Salamis and Ventouris Sea Line's* **Panagia Tinou 2** *arriving from the Cyclades.*

The pressure of berths at Piraeus can find 25 and more ships alongside in the early hours of the morning and with the close competition between operators requiring them to run their services at very similar departure times, the procession of vessels leaving between seven thirty and nine thirty each morning in high summer is quite extraordinary in the eyes of a visitor more used to the orderly clockwork operations at regular intervals in the English Channel and northern Europe. Equally the lines of ships berthed beside one another with no intervening piers and often no more than five metres apart initially gives an impression rather of a collection of retired ferries from a previous generation than the hub of this most efficient transport system.

or the final call to the scrap yard. In the shipyards of Perama and Elefsis new construction and major rebuilding of vessels that have started their lives elsewhere renews and refreshes the Greek fleet. A visually ugly town, largely flattened by the retreating Germans in 1944 and since overwhelmed by the cement buildings that are a characteristic of modern Greece, Piraeus remains the centre of the Greek ferry system.

Entering from the sea two moles protect the Great Harbour. That to the north disappears through a cement works to the dull suburb of Drapetsona, while that to the south forms part of a large naval college and dockyard which continues to mount prominent displays of anti-aircraft artillery and with its walls endlessly patrolled by navy sentries. The north shore contains a number of berths used for vessels laying by (it was here that the fleet of Ventouris Sea Lines was laid-up following the collapse of the company in 1995) and a pair of modest

The Great Harbour is well supplied with transport connections with the termini of both of Greece's railway systems – the station for the standard gauge network to Thessalonika and on through the Balkans to the rest of Europe within 100 metres of the departure points of the ferries to Crete, while the metre gauge system around the Peloponnese has its terminus in the north-eastern corner of the harbour, adjacent to the impressive station of the electric railway – the

Above: *Agapitos Lines'* **Naias Express** *arriving in Piraeus.*

underground railway of Athens – providing a regular service into the centre of the capital, it will eventually be incorporated in a new metro network to much of the metropolitan area, the construction of which has occupied much of the second half of the 1990s with enormous noise and disruption to those living in and visiting Athens. Frequent bus services from Athens and the surrounding area, including the airport at Hellenikon, terminate in the central block of the harbour in between the ferries to the Cyclades.

At the centre of the Great Harbour, beside the bus station, can be found a block containing praktoreions selling tickets to destinations throughout the Aegean. The commission-driven salesmen in these offices and busking outside them make great efforts to indicate that they are unique sources of wisdom on forthcoming departures and have bargain fares, but in reality almost all of the offices sell tickets for almost all of the lines and, fares being strictly regulated by the government, provide no advantage over one another or the more civilised offices maintained by the shipping companies along Akti Miaouli. The Greek enthusiasm for neon and other illuminated signs reaches its apogee on the walls of this block, with almost every square inch taken with flashing

Right: *A typical line of ferries loading for Crete in the Great Harbour in 1999 – Minoan Lines'* **King Minos,** *ANEK's* **Aptera,** *LANE's recently acquired* **Ierapetra** *and Minoan's ro-ro* **Agia Galini.**

advertisements for the competing charms of the different lines. Whether or not they influence the choice of any potential travellers, they inspire awe on the bleary-eyed traveller stumbling onto the port after a charter flight has deposited him at Athens' overcrowded airport at Hellenikon in the small hours, and seem to induce some of the more improbable decisions on future holiday plans made by first-time visitors to the country.

Access to all of the quays within the Great Harbour is open and unrestricted. There is little standage room for vehicular traffic, but vehicles usually time their arrival after boarding of the ferry ships commences and the familiarity of Greek drivers with the quays from which the different services depart means that, without apparent organisation, embarkation will take place smoothly and efficiently. Despite the increasing introduction of more modern vessels, many ferries still sailing from Piraeus were built at a time when traffic was a fraction of its current level and accordingly have

Map 4:
Piraeus and the Saronic Gulf

GULF OF CORINTH

- - - - - Railway

Rafina

Megara

Elefsis

Perama

Piraeus

ATHENS

Spata Airport
(under construction)

SALAMIS

Hellenikon
Airport

CORINTH CANAL

ATTICA

AEGINA

SARONIC GULF

Lavrion

0   5 km

0   5 miles

CAPE SOUNION

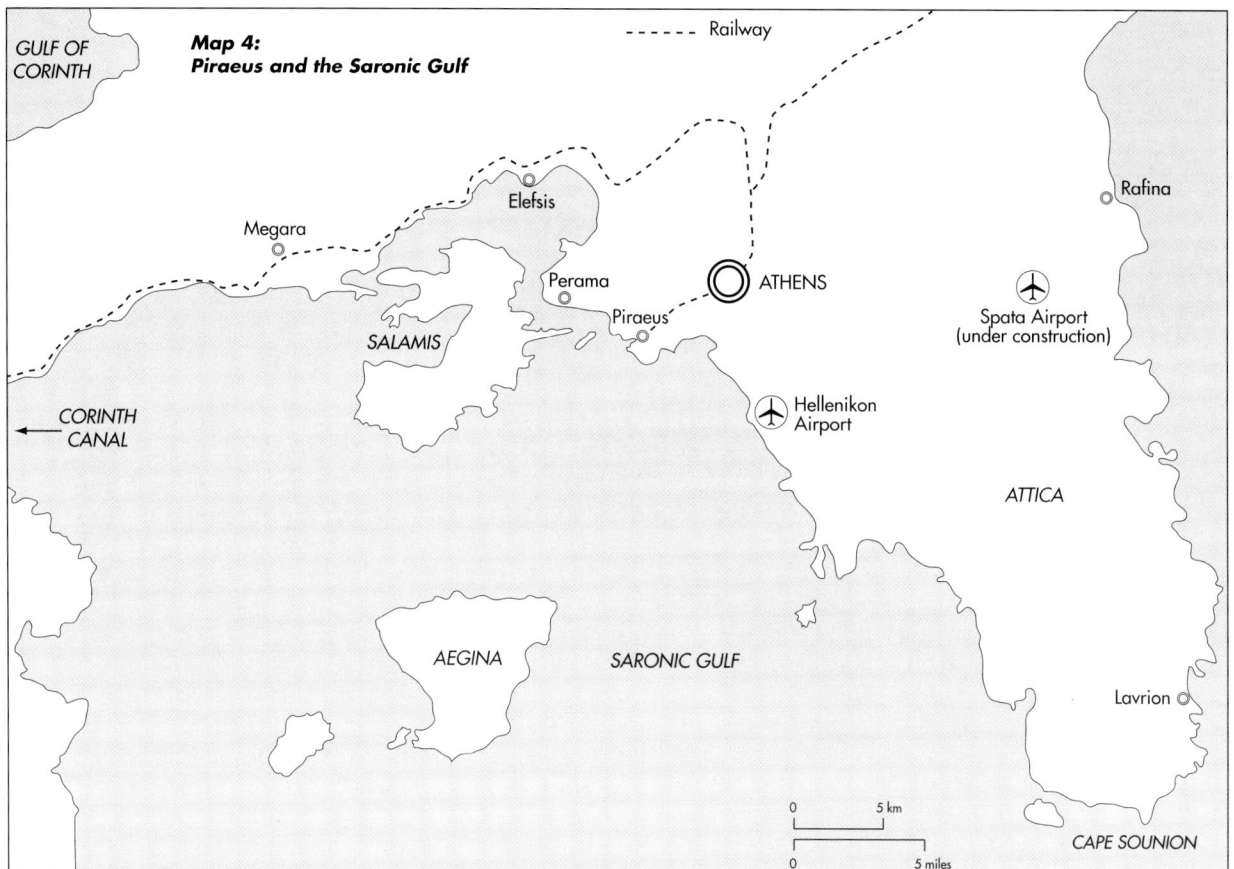

small and cramped stern doors. The process of loading large vehicles and their trailers and separating them into appropriate parts of the vehicle deck to suit the intermediate ports of call requires careful management, accomplished without any apparent recourse to computers or other more modern forms of planning but simply willpower, shouting and much waving of arms. Foot passengers will mill around on the quayside, usually having to board over the vehicle ramp amidst the exhaust and spinning wheels of freight traffic being loaded before climbing steel stairways within the ship to reach the open decks above. As usual the contribution of the port police to the proceedings is hard to gauge and, since they are clearly too important to give advice or directions to travellers seeking their vessel, is better appreciated as a piece of theatre then an attempt to control or assist travellers.

South of the central block from which the Cyclades ferries depart is a slipway used by the regular landing craft ferries on the services to Aegina. As with similar services elsewhere, several of them will be at quayside at any hour of the day or night, with one loading and others awaiting their turn, dozing in the sunshine, and with the portholes closed against the noxious smells of the harbour in which a lack of tides and the detritus of tens of thousands of travellers daily, can leave a discouraging fragrance to assault the nostrils.

At the corner of the Great Harbour (quay 9 on Map 5) can be found some of the more improbable craft serving Piraeus, motorboats derived from caiques running to the nearby island of Salamis (see Chapter 13). Bobbing through the harbour full of enormous ferries and cruise ships with apparently unsilenced two-stroke engines, they demonstrate the inherent lack of respect to greatness which is one of the more charming characteristics of the Greek people. Despite the lack of attraction in their destination, they also provide one of the best grandstands to see both the operations in the Great Harbour and the vessels at quays and anchorages between

Piraeus, Perama and Salamis.

Immediately adjoining is an area given over to the hydrofoils of Flying Dolphin and of Sea Falcon lines operating regularly to Aegina, with more occasional visits from other fast ferries on the same service. The spider-like underwater foils of the Flying Dolphins creeping through the Great Harbour with its ever-changing variety of vessels add yet another dimension to this most fascinating of ports.

The southern side of the harbour has a small area fenced off for ferries on international services but, as noted in Chapter 12, these form a comparatively minor part of the operations in the Aegean and the quays are more usually deserted for days at a stretch. They immediately adjoin the cruise terminals at which up to half a dozen cruise vessels will often be berthed at the beginning or end of Mediterranean cruises or simply visiting in the course of journeys from other ports. The enormous contrast between these large entertainment centres and the purposeful ferries sailing around Greece demonstrates the broad range of modern passenger shipping.

On the other side of the Piraeus peninsula is the port of Zea, home for much of the year to the ostentatious yachts and motor cruisers of the Athenian business elite and surrounded by apartments which present an air of prosperity lacking in many parts of the city. At the seaward end of the harbour is a small terminal, around which up to a dozen Russian-built hydrofoils from the Flying Dolphins fleet will be dispersed, waiting their turn on services to the Saronic Gulf. The regular rush of passengers between the two terminals of Flying Dolphins gives rise to much excitement for the local taxi-drivers.

Returning to the north and passing the Great Harbour entrance and on through the straits of Salamis (see Chapter 13) brings one to the anchorage of Elefsis (see Map 4), the preferred location for the lay-up of vessels from the Greek fleet. Amongst unemployed super-tankers and superannuated

Above: *A line of ferries 'Mediterranean moored' at Piraeus in 1995. The* **Vitsentzos Kornaros, Rethimnon, Knossos, Theseus, Milos Express** *and* **Apollo Express 2**.

cruise vessels can usually be found twenty or more redundant ferries, some of which have passed the 35-year limit on vessels operating under the Greek flag as well as newer vessels which can expect renewed activity when a suitable niche reopens in the market. A notable long-term resident in the late 1990s has been DFDS' stalwart of the 1960s and '70s the *England* which has travelled far and wide after withdrawal from North Sea operations without finding a secure new home. Almost entirely surrounded by mountains, and with narrow entrances providing little current to disturb the ships, Elefsis provides one of the best and safest anchorages in the Mediterranean. The National Road heading for the Peloponnese skirts the northern shores of the Bay of Elefsis and provides glimpses of the ships, many of which are chained together, with ten or more vessels in lines beside one another. At the western end of the bay is the unmistakable shape of the former Union-Castle liner *Windsor Castle*, owned by Greek ship-owners since withdrawal in 1978 and, after use as an accommodation vessel in Saudi Arabia, laid-up here for more than fifteen years. Whether or not she will ever sail again, she presents a lovely profile off one of the few attractive parts of the island of Salamis.

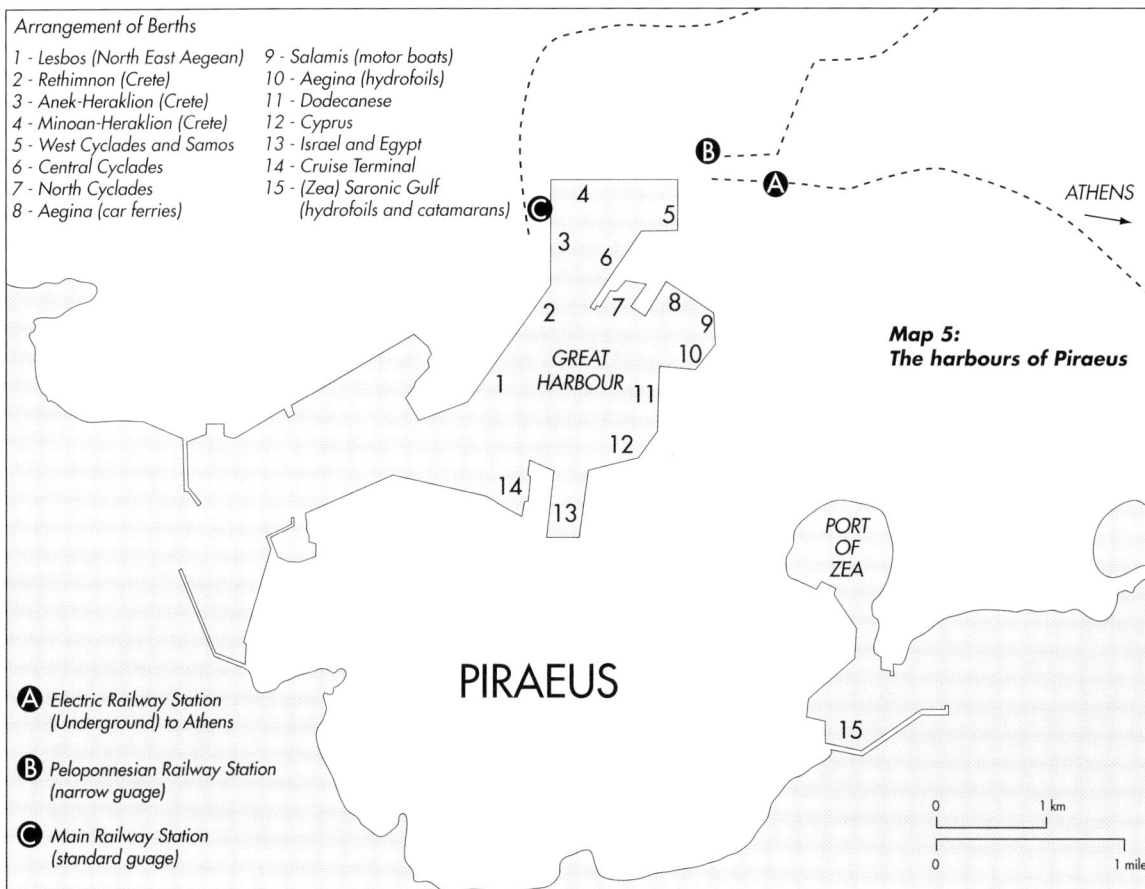

Arrangement of Berths

1 - Lesbos (North East Aegean)
2 - Rethimnon (Crete)
3 - Anek-Heraklion (Crete)
4 - Minoan-Heraklion (Crete)
5 - West Cyclades and Samos
6 - Central Cyclades
7 - North Cyclades
8 - Aegina (car ferries)
9 - Salamis (motor boats)
10 - Aegina (hydrofoils)
11 - Dodecanese
12 - Cyprus
13 - Israel and Egypt
14 - Cruise Terminal
15 - (Zea) Saronic Gulf (hydrofoils and catamarans)

Map 5:
The harbours of Piraeus

ATHENS →

GREAT HARBOUR

PIRAEUS

PORT OF ZEA

Ⓐ Electric Railway Station (Underground) to Athens

Ⓑ Peloponnesian Railway Station (narrow guage)

Ⓒ Main Railway Station (standard guage)

0   1 km

0   1 mile

Aegean Ports

Chapter 16

Rafina

Although Piraeus is the principal port of Athens, Rafina is also easily accessible from the capital, 30 kilometres along one of the capital's less daunting roads, and linked to it by a half-hourly bus service. From here the majority of the ferries to the northern Cyclades depart, as well as some of the routes to Evia and occasional longer-distance services to the north-eastern Aegean.

Rafina is a pleasant port from which to travel. Here in place of the bustle and grime of Piraeus the praktoreions share the harbour front with fish restaurants outside which lines of octopus are hung to season and the inevitable Greek coffee shops serve small cups of immensely strong coffee to a mainly male clientele.

Until 1998 it was the scene of the shared operation by a consortium of Agoudimos, Strintzis and Ventouris Ferries operating a co-ordinated service and sharing the busier weekend savings with quieter mid-week runs in an effort to balance revenue and time in port. The expansionist policies of Strintzis, necessitated by its stock market listing and the urge to improve on the previous year's performance, combined with the financial weakness of Ventouris Ferries (which led to the sale of its operation to Agapitos Ferries at the end of the year) saw this collapse during 1998. Firstly, Strintzis introduced an independent operation using the much-travelled *Ionian Sun* appearing to run in competition with the consortium's own sailings and the subsequent acquisition of the other shares in

the jointly owned *Sea Jet 1* catamaran have led to a changed set of circumstances since 1999. Co-operation does however continue in reduced form between Agoudimos and Agapitos Express in competition with both Strintzis and Goutos Lines. The summer of 1999 saw some mornings when seven ferries and fast craft left the port between half past seven and nine o'clock for the same group of islands, which were surely not capable of sustaining such a volume of traffic and reductions in frequency will inevitably occur.

Never a member of the consortium and offering increased competition with its growing fleet of fast and semi-fast catamarans, Goutos Lines operate similar services to the north Cyclades. The previously fairly sleepy operations out of Rafina are now in a period of far more intense competition and between them provide excellent examples of each generation of ferry (apart from the new style of ro-pax) to be found in Greek waters.

Rafina bustles with activity early in the mornings and again in the evenings as the ships which have departed in the morning for the most distant parts return and reload for night crossings while those on the shorter crossings to Evia and Andros make their more regular appearance. The peace of the port after the heat and pollution of central Athens makes this a popular evening retreat for residents in the capital and the fares, traditionally 20% below those applying from Piraeus, ensure that this pleasant town has a prominent place in the ferry timetables.

Above: *The **Penelope A** arriving at Rafina with her stern door almost fully lowered and members of the crew at the extreme end of it ready to assist in the berthing.*

Right: *A busy evening at Rafina in 1998 as the* **Express Karistos** *arrives from Evia, while in the background the Agoudimos Lines* **Penelope A** *approaches from Mykonos and, in the far distance, Mykonos A.N.E.'s* **Mykonos II** *approaches on a freight sailing.*

Volos

In a bay opposite the northern part of the island of Evia and the principal mainland port for services to the Sporades, Volos also sees calls by vessels on the long routes between Thessalonika and Crete. Volos had a significant maritime role in Greece until destroyed by earthquakes in 1954 and 1955. The rebuilding in a typical cement style has not produced a town of great beauty and much of the former maritime significance has departed. Well connected by train and bus services to Athens and much of central Greece, if the town itself lacks charm its location under the beautiful and heavily wooded Mount Pelion and the narrow approaches through the Gulf and around the northern end of Evia make this a delightful port to sail from and in summer it sees around half a dozen ferry departures per day together with a similar number of visits by Flying Dolphins. The latter also travel much further up the Evia Channel to the small town of Ayios Konstantinos to make connections with express buses on the National Road to Athens.

Thessalonika

Most northerly of the principal mainland ports of the Aegean is Thessalonika, chief city of the Greek province of Macedonia and enjoying a cultural life that is as different from the capital as is that of Edinburgh from London. A military centre since the days of Alexander the Great, whose capital at Vergina was 75 kilometres to the west, it has housed the headquarters for NATO in south-east Europe since the Second World War and during the recent conflicts in the Balkans has been used as the principal supply port for the ground forces.

Although immensely welcoming to visitors, Greece has tended to view its neighbours to the north and east with emotions between open hostility and armed neutrality throughout its independent history. The Yugoslav republic of Macedonia to the north has a particular thorn in the side of Greek Governments of the 1980s and 1990s and with the collapse of the political union in

Yugoslavia a movement to 'reunite' that republic with Greece has enjoyed considerable political support in Athens. While there has been no evidence that the inhabitants have wished to share it, it has added to the tensions of Greece's relationship with her neighbours and nowhere is this more apparent than in Thessalonika.

Ferries leave from the western end of the extensive harbour overlooked by the dreary architecture of the city (the result of another earthquake in 1978) but which includes some of Greece's most interesting museums. Daily services by Flying Dolphins to the Sporades are joined by twice weekly visits from the NEL fleet from Lesbos and Chios, a single weekly visit from Rhodes by DANE (which did not operate in 1998) and visits on alternate days by the *El Greco* of Minoan Lines and the *Dimitroula* of GA Ferries on their competing services to Heraklion in Crete, at 555 kilometres distance the longest domestic ferry routes in Greece. An interesting city with a spacious port, it seems likely that it will grow in importance as a ferry port as the islands of the north-eastern Aegean develop.

Right: *The RMT sisters of the mid-1970s have been reunited at Rafina in 1999. The former* **Prins Philippe** *of 1973 was rebuilt in her stern superstructure and funnel before taking up service with Agapitos Express Ferries as their* **Express Athina** *running through the northern Cyclades to Mykonos.*

Chapter 17

The Operators

Agapitos Lines

Previously trading as Agapitos Brothers, the family run company is involved in services throughout the Cyclades and into the northern Aegean, as well as having one vessel participating in the Corfu consortium (see Chapter 10). Run from offices in central Piraeus, it has operated a varied and fascinating fleet down the years and until 1999 ran six vessels all in late middle age. Well turned out and generally busy, the fleet may lack the glamour of some of the larger operators with access to stock market funds, but appears well equipped to operate in its chosen market and has been joined in late 1999 by a new passenger fast craft.

Among the last Greek operators of turbine steamships,

Above: *Little altered from her days as SNCF's last turbine passenger ship on the Newhaven to Dieppe service, Agapitos Line's **Apollon** gets underway from Piraeus in 1980 when on a daily service to Paros, Naxos and Mykonos – shortly before the end of steam ship services in the Greek Islands.*

Above: *After finding the ticket that you want and locating your ferry, the process of boarding can be noisy and confusing - loading the **Milos Express** with pedestrians, reversing cars, food vendors and much whistle blowing.*

their *Apollon* – originally SNCF's *Lisieux* from Newhaven to Dieppe service – remained in operation until 1981, the fleet has subsequently settled on medium sized car ferries of which the oldest pair are now *Golden Vergina* and *Naias II*, a pair of twins who have worked together throughout their lives, half-sisters to the *Nuits St Georges* which became the first car ferry to serve Ramsgate. Originally built in France for service in the SNCM fleet, they joined Agapitos in 1982 and 1983. Although regularly encountering one another in the Great Harbour at Piraeus, their services are very different with the *Golden Vergina* running the long service to Ikaria and Samos – a twelve-hour crossing – whilst the *Naias II* runs daily to Syros, Tinos and Mykonos in the central Cyclades – a voyage of no more than six hours. Although relatively elegant from the exterior, with an unmistakably French profile, their interiors are by no means comfortable and by far the best way to travel is on their spacious open decks – the interior is better reserved in case an escape is needed from the baking sun of a July afternoon.

In contrast, the *Naias Express* is a ship with an interesting history and far better internal accommodation. Built in Italy for British Rail as the *Ailsa Princess* for the Stranraer-Larne service in 1971, she later operated from Weymouth and during Sealink's final phase in the Channel Island services was renamed as the *Earl Harold* until sale in 1989. She had a spell with GA Ferries as their *Dimitra* during which her stern superstructure was extended but little other external work was carried out. Following

Above: *Agapitos Lines' **Panagia Ekatontapyliani** basking in the sun at Piraeus on an August afternoon in 1999. Despite alterations to her superstructure at the stern to increase accommodation for deck class passengers, she remains easily recognisable as British Rail's **Hengist**.*

sale to Agapitos in 1995 she was further rebuilt with an extended forward superstructure and a notably sharp bow replacing the curved bow visor with which she had been built. Her service continues beyond Mykonos through the small islands of the eastern Cyclades at weekly intervals, one of many examples in the Aegean of uneconomic services required by the Ministry of Shipping as a condition for the operating licence on her far more profitable route to Mykonos.

The Japanese-built *Super Naias* spent twenty years with ANEK as their *Kriti* before joining Agapitos in 1997. The straight lines of her hull give an unmistakable indication of her initial purpose as a Japanese train ferry and subsequent re-buildings have failed to provide very luxurious passenger accommodation, although she does have considerable outside deck space. In addition to regular services through the southern Cyclades to Santorini she also pays weekly visits around some of the eastern Cyclades. The name *Naias* is the ancient word for a nymph – a description which singularly poorly fits this ugly but capacious ship.

Above: *When first sold to Greece in 1991, the former Sealink* **Earl Granville** *operated for Agapitos Lines with a plain white hull as* **Express Olympia***, in which guise she is seen leaving Piraeus. Since 1993 she has sailed in the colours of Agapitos Express*

With a name apparently designed to exercise the tonsils, but in reality taken from the name of the Cathedral on the island of Paros to which she provides one of the principal links, the *Panagia Ekatontapyliani* is none other than Sealink's one-time *Hengist*. With a reputation as the fastest of the conventional vessels currently serving the central Cyclades, an important factor in winning trade from local travellers and important to holiday makers arriving in crowded islands with a need to find accommodation on arrival, she is well maintained and smartly run. After the closure of the Folkestone to Boulogne service she was sold in 1992 and she initially served with Ventouris Sea Lines as their *Apollon Express 2* operating with her sister ship *Senlac* (now the *Express Apollon*) and spent the summer of 1996 laid-up in Piraeus pending sale by her mortgagees to Agapitos at a very favourable price for a ship of her capacity and type.

In July 1999 the company announced that it had purchased its first high-speed craft, a 52-metre FBM Tri-Cat to be named *Sea Speed I*. Capable of 45 knots and carrying 447 passengers, her entry into service was delayed by the

inevitable bureaucracy of obtaining an operating licence from the Ministry but represents a further step in the spread of fast ferry services in Greek waters.

Agapitos Express

Established in 1993, the second ferry business of the Agapitos family has followed a similar line to the older established company. Operating a splendidly interesting fleet of seven ships in the Aegean, principally in the Cyclades services, it is one of the most impressive of the current Greek ferry operators. Financed by a combination of capital provided by its family shareholders and bank borrowing it has eschewed the allure of the Athens stock market and as a result has retained an ability to react quickly and unpredictably, to the great benefit of its proprietors and the passengers it serves.

Beginning with a pair of vessels on the long service through the central and southern Cyclades to Paros, Naxos, Ios and Santorini, the company greatly benefited from the collapse of Ventouris Sea Lines and the dismemberment of its fleet to acquire a dominant position in the Cyclades trades.

The first vessel in the fleet, after a short spell with Agapitos Brothers, was the *Express Olympia*, one of the series of compact ferries built by Meyer Werft at Papenburg in the early 1970s for members of the Viking Line consortium. After initial Baltic service as the *Viking 4* she was acquired by Sealink in 1980 and sailed as their *Earl Granville* for the whole of the 1980s. Largely associated with the Channel Islands services from Portsmouth, she was refitted in 1985 for the catastrophic 'Bateau de Luxe' experiment which raised fares and considerably enhanced standards in a business which required neither and rapidly failed with the unexpected competition from Channel Islands Ferries. Sold in 1990, she initially entered service with a plain white hull and the traditional 'AA' funnel design of the Agapitos Brothers fleet before transfer to her new operators under the charismatic

Above: *Originally SNCF's* **Chartres***, the* **Express Santorini** *of Agapitos Express Ferries seen on an unusually clear morning with the island of Aegina in the distance.*

Above: *The **Naias Express** at Piraeus on a warm night in 1996. The one time Sealink **Ailsa Princess** has served in Greece since 1989 and her superstructure has been progressively extended at the stern and then the bow.*

presidency of John Agapitos. Modest in size by modern standards, she manages a passenger certificate for 1,200, only 198 of whom can be berthed. Conditions in deck class when approaching her full capacity can be daunting and on the day that the Piraeus Port Police carried out their notorious (and apparently unique) inspection of numbers to reveal almost 2,200 aboard led to the introduction of the no doubt well intentioned but unevenly applied computerised reservation system which all operators are now supposed to use.

Her normal running mate on the route to Santorini is the *Express Santorini* – built as SNCF's *Chartres* in 1974 for operation as a train ferry between Dover and Dunkerque and also on the car ferry service from Calais. Subsequent changes of livery and a spell on the Newhaven to Dieppe service brought her to a final period on the rail-connected sailings between Dover Marine and Calais and it was she that closed this historic route on 24th September 1993. She was very quickly snapped up by Agapitos Express and has retained much for internal fittings from her service on the Straits of Dover. Her operations are generally balanced with those of the *Express Olympia* with daily departures at eight in the morning from both Piraeus and Santorini – albeit with occasional services through the lesser islands of the chain in mid-week to satisfy the terms of their operating licences.

The admirable trio of car ferries built for Sealink at the Brest Naval Dockyard in 1972/3 have all come to work in the Aegean in the 1990s. The last to be introduced, the *Senlac* entered service in 1973 on the Newhaven to Dieppe service, being transferred to the SNCF fleet following the withdrawal of the British operator from the route in 1985. In 1987 she was chartered to B&I Line for a season on the Fishguard to Rosslare link at the end of which she was sold to Ventouris Sea Lines as their *Apollon Express* (*Apollon Express 1* after the acquisition of the former *Hengist* in 1991). Operating a daily service to Santorini returning overnight, her accommodation was slightly extended at the stern but otherwise little altered from its distinctive profile and she appeared to be one of the most successful units of the Ventouris operation until its sudden demise. Rapidly

repossessed by the bank that had provided the finance to acquire her, she was quickly resold to Agapitos Express and slightly renamed to her current style of *Express Apollon* for operation during the 1996 summer season. She runs slightly slower than her former fleet mate in the Agapitos Lines fleet but this does nothing to impede the vast numbers of foreign holidaymakers who travel on her each year or the quantities of freight that are transported to and from the islands that she serves.

Another former Ventouris vessel to have joined the fleet but operating on a rather different service in the Saronic Gulf, the *Express Danae* is unique in the fleet for having been built in Greece. After spending the 1970s and early '80s sailing for Agapitos Lines as the *Kyklades* serving the smaller items of the eastern Cyclades, she entered a long period of lay up before purchase by Ventouris, renamed as the *Methodia* and placed on the long route from Piraeus to Porto Heli via Hydra. Following the Ventouris collapse she was acquired by Agapitos Express and continues to run in the same service – an elegant ship for her size but rather dated by comparison to the larger vessels in the fleet.

The introduction of the HSS craft on the Stena Line

Above: *Agapitos Express Ferries' **Express Athina** awaits her sailing time from Rafina as tourists enjoy the sun.*

service from Holyhead to Dun Laoghaire in 1996 spelt the beginning of the end of the long-standing railway ferry between the ports. The last conventional vessel on the route, built as the *St. Columba* and renamed in 1991 as the *Stena Hibernia* spent a final season as the *Stena Adventurer* before sale in spring 1997 to Agapitos Express. Little altered from her service on the Irish Sea apart from the inevitable small extensions to the stern superstructure, she operates a simple daily return service leaving Piraeus at eight fifteen every morning for Syros, Tinos and Mykonos. She remains in excellent condition

Above: *Agoudimos Lines'* **Penelope A** *on her regular service between Mykonos and Rafina.*

and carries heavy loadings of freight as well as fully employing her passenger certificate of 1,700.

Relatively unsuccessful with her original operators RMT, the *Prins Philippe* of 1973 ran until 1985 but was eventually made redundant from the Dover to Ostend service due to her lack of freight capacity and fixed mezzanine deck. However her sturdy engines and comfortable passenger accommodation saw her joining the Italian fleet of Moby Lines in 1986. Her career as the *Moby Love* lasted until 1993 when she was sold to Ventouris Sea Lines by when her funnel had been somewhat altered and her superstructure extended. She replaced the former Zeeland Steamship Company's *Koningin Wilhelmina* in the fleet where she had served as the *Panagia Tinou*, the last large classic ferry in Greek waters but by then uncompetitive due to her lack of car capacity. Her replacement took her name with the suffix 'II' in 1993 and operated very successfully until the ending of the company's operations. Whereas some of the creditors of the Ventouris company forced quick sales on the vessels in the fleet, the National Bank of Greece who had made the loan on this vessel kept her in operation through 1996, albeit without any significant maintenance work. She spent 1997 in a run down condition laid-up in the Great Harbour in Piraeus close to the cruise terminal but in 1998 was acquired by Agapitos Express, refitted within the Great Harbour and introduced to service on 1st August as the *Express Athina* on a further permutation of services to Syros, Mykonos, Naxos and Paros. In 1999 she took over the operations at Rafina which were previously the preserve of the *Bari Express*, running in competition with Strintzis' *Superferry II* – her sister ship and one-time fleetmate *Prince Laurent*.

The joint operations out of Rafina have been described above and from 1990 these included the operation of another former member of the RMT fleet, the lovely *Princesse Astrid* of 1968. Last of her generation of Belgian vessels, her limited vehicle capacity saw her withdrawal at the end of the 1983 season and purchase by Ventouris Ferries. Converted with a small forward sundeck and modest extension to her aft superstructure, she entered service in 1984 as the *Bari Express* running from that Italian port to Patras. Replaced by larger tonnage on that route (see Chapter 10) she moved to start a new operation from Rafina to the northern Cyclades of Andros, Tinos and Mykonos. A noticeably successful ship on this route, her operations were unchanged until the end of the 1998 season when Ventouris Ferries underwent a period of contraction. This led to the sale of this fine vessel and perhaps even more importantly its operating licence to Agapitos Express by whom she has been renamed *Express Hermes*. In 1999 she exchanged places with the *Express Athina* and operated a five times weekly service out of Piraeus among the eastern Cyclades.

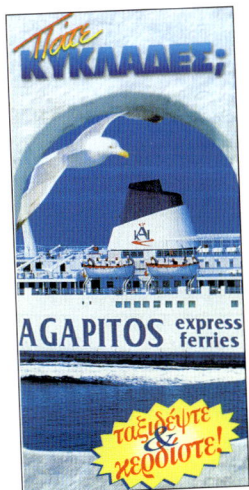

Agoudimos Lines

Although continuing to operate in the Adriatic (see Chapter 10) the principal focus of Agoudimos Lines has been centred in Rafina throughout the 1990s. Initially operating with the *Kapetan Alexandros A*, the company was looking for a larger vessel at the time that Sealink announced its intention to withdraw the Folkestone to Boulogne service. The chairman of the company travelled to the UK and was a passenger on the memorable final voyage on New Year's Eve 1991 operated, at the instigation of Ferry Publications, by the *Stena Horsa*. These crossings are credited with settling on the choice of vessel and the ship was rapidly sold to Agoudimos. Rapidly converted with minimal external operations in Greece (even her lounge for use by Orient Express passengers was retained) she remains the best of the ferries sailing out of Rafina and a credit to her operators.

Above: *ANEK's Japanese-built **Aptera**, used for many years on the Piraeus to Crete services, preparing to sail.*

Amorgos Ferries

The operator of two small car ferries in the southern Cyclades, Amorgos Ferries is one of the few companies specialising in inter-island services rather than aiming for connections to the mainland. The older of the pair is the *Express Paros* built at Perama in 1965 and employed until 1994 by Strintzis as their *Kefalonia* before she was replaced by the Japanese vessel that now carries the name on the service from Patras to the Ionian Islands. Unusual for her total lack of funnel and cramped passenger accommodation beside rather than above the vehicle deck she is an ugly and rather slow vessel but carrying on an important and useful service. Her running mate, the *Syros Express* was also built in Greece and has a far more attractive profile. After initial operation in the Aegean, she spent several seasons competing on the service from Corfu to Igoumenitsa before being transferred to her current operators.

ANEK (the Shipping Company of Crete)

Until the 1960s ferry companies in Greece tended to be controlled from Piraeus by a succession of powerful ship owning families. In 1968 the concept of a ferry company based on an island it was founded to serve and with its shareholding widely distributed amongst the island people was established when ANEK, the Shipping Company of Crete was established. To the chagrin of its detractors the company has remained consistently profitable and has grown steadily and rapidly to be one of the largest operators of ferry ships in Greek waters.

Having long enjoyed a reputation for shrewd purchases in the second-hand market, particularly in Japan, ANEK launched themselves onto the Athens stock market at the end of 1998 to raise US $67 million of initial extra capital, with the prospect of a further share issue to follow. The proceeds are to be invested both by placing orders for two new ships (for the Adriatic) and by the acquisition of shareholdings in DANE, LANE and NEL, and the purchase of Cretan Ferries (as to all of which, see below). Despite its status as a public company, 75% of the shareholders are resident in Crete and the chairman of the company is the Metropolitan Archbishop of Western Crete – truly a local business that has secured a large role in the Greek ferry business.

The company's own operations in the Aegean have remained relatively consistent throughout this period with three routes from Piraeus to the home island of Crete, running to the island capital of Heraklion and to ANEK's home port of Chania and the western port of Kastelli Kissamou. For long appearing to operate in the shadow of Minoan Lines, the company is now beginning to plough a very different furrow, with far more controlled borrowings and a more limited issue of shares, but little serious sign of the replacement of the ageing fleet which must cause increasing anxiety as the implementation of the latest SOLAS regulations in 2002 approaches.

Long-standing stalwarts on the Piraeus to Heraklion service, the Japanese-built sisters *Candia* and *Rethimnon* joined the company's fleet in 1972, when both were only one year old. With comparatively modest accommodation for only 470 passengers in berths (almost all in four-berth cabins), the balance of their 1,500 passenger certificate is contributed by deck class passengers, not entirely satisfactory for vessels operating almost exclusively on overnight passages. The arrival of later vessels with larger numbers of cabins have steadily relegated the two ships from front-line duties. In 1997 and 1998 the *Candia* operated the route from Piraeus to Kastelli Kissamou in western Crete before being taken on charter by DANE in 1999, after ANEK had taken a 40% interest in the Dodecanese operator. In the interim her sister has continued to operate to Heraklion, but the prospect of the new Minoan vessels now building in South Korea have sent the company back to the second-hand market to look for a more appropriate form of vessel with which to continue the competition without incurring the substantial expense of new construction.

Running-mate of the *Rethimnon* on the service to Heraklion is the *Aptera*, a far larger Japanese-built vessel with cabin space for a significantly higher percentage of passengers.

The two vessels running on the service to Chania are the *Lato* and the *Lissos*. So spectacularly hideous as to prompt speculation that the naval architect responsible was hallucinating from some terrible affliction when preparing their design, the pair nonetheless provide considerable capacity within their vehicle decks and passenger accommodation but their narrow stern doors appear to limit their turnaround in port on days when daylight as well as overnight crossings are provided. The *Lato* was built as a sister ship of the vessel now sailing for Minoan in the Adriatic as the *Erotokritos*. Some 188 metres in length, the uneven profile and side ramps at her bow conspire to produce a perfectly hideous but entirely effective mover of freight and passengers while her running mate the *Lissos* is an even more serious affront to the eye.

Finally, ANEK's operations include a unique annual cruise around the Aegean in December using the enormous *El Venizelos* from the Adriatic service. The itinerary changes each year but brings this enormous vessel into small island ports such as Syros which it totally overwhelms even before the capacity load of Greek travellers descend onto the quayside.

Arkadia Lines

The sudden spectacular growth, relatively brief zenith, and rapid decline of ship-owning companies are relatively commonplace features of Greek shipping operations. One of the clearer examples of this in the Aegean ferry scene is Arkadia Lines. Newly established at the end of the 1980s, it blossomed with the purchase of the Shipping Company of Naxos with its two small car ferries *Naxos* and *Paros*, and the growth of operations on the Adriatic routes. From a peak of six vessels, the company now operates just a single craft in the highly-lucrative Cyclades services to Santorini.

The relatively small sisters were replaced in 1991 by the *Poseidon Express* – previously SNCM's *Provence*. A far larger ship, with greatly-enhanced passenger accommodation and vehicle capacity, she was for her time the best ship in the Cyclades services. Competition increased, the company's operations in the Adriatic were hampered by constantly-changing vessels, and ultimately the onset of old age in the *Silver Paloma*, the one-time Deutsche Reichsbahn train ferry *Sassnitz* built in 1959 to operate to Trelleborg in Sweden. Her retirement coincided with damage to the *Poseidon Express* when she was holed at Paros in early 1996, endeavouring to avoid a collision with the *Naias Express*. Although no passengers were injured and the vehicles on board were all unloaded, the ship subsequently capsized. This led the company to switch its interesting *Dimitrios Express* at short notice from the Adriatic to the more profitable Cyclades route, where she was rapidly renamed the *Poseidon Express 2*. Built in 1973 to operate for Irish Continental Lines as their *Saint Patrick* and later renamed as the *Saint Colum 1* for the associated Belfast Car Ferries, her accommodation was extended spectacularly but not elegantly both at the stern and above the bridge forward. Despite this, she has proved to be a remarkably effective ferry in the Aegean.

Arsinoi

The company operates a single vessel from Kavala to the northern island of Samothrace. The *Arsinoi* is an unattractive

Above: *One of the two smartly liveried vessels of Cretan Ferries on the service from Piraeus to Rethimnon, the **Preveli** is seen bunkering at the mainland port.*

Above: *At speed in the Saronic Gulf on her way to Piraeus from Rhodes in the summer of 1997, the unusually elegant Japanese-built **Rodos** of DANE Sea Lines.*

vessel but retains a feature which was once commonplace among Greek ferries which has tended to be usurped by commercial pressures – a Greek Orthodox chapel, complete with icons and sanctuary lamp. She seems well able to cope with the sometimes tempestuous seas of the northern Aegean but it is felt necessary to continue the provision of such a facility despite an excellent safety record.

Cretan Ferries (Rethimnaki Shipping Company)

Although the largest Greek island, the existence of four separate ferry services from Piraeus to ports along the northern coast of the 250-kilometre long island is commented upon in Chapter 13. There is considerable rivalry between the western part of the island around Chania and the capital of Heraklion but the introduction of a ferry service to Rethimnon, the third city of the island, in 1989 caused some surprise. The continuance of the route on a daily basis has demonstrated as much the enormous demand for travel between Crete and the mainland as the need for the existence of this separate service. The two vessels used, the *Arkadi* and the *Preveli* take their names from prominent monasteries on the island with important roles in the independence movement from Turkey during the 19th century. Both are smartly turned out and offer remarkably comfortable accommodation for their comparatively modest size. Both continue to operate single nightly sailings in each direction and appear to do comfortable but unspectacular business. In May 1999 the company was taken over by ANEK and, although there has been little obvious sign of change during the early period of the merger, it seems likely that the identity of the company and the livery of the ships will be subsumed by the new parent, with the likelihood of redeployment of the vessels in due course to help with the modernisation of the fleet elsewhere.

DANE (the Dodecanese Shipping Company)

Long established as one of the two principal operators between Piraeus and the Dodecanese, the Rhodes-based company appeared to have a sound and successful business when it was launched onto the Athens stock market in 1996. Unfortunately, by late 1997 rumours of financial malpractice combined with disappointing results, led to a collapse in share values, leading to a suspension in trading of the shares and repeated rumours of impending collapse. With the aid of its bankers the company struggled on through the 1998 season, surviving even the severe damage by fire of the *Leros* on 12th

Above: *ANEK's Candia seen on charter to DANE in 1999.*

Above: *Showing the revised livery introduced in 1999 after the merger with Minoan Lines, the* **Flying Dolphin VIII** *is berthed ahead of a sister craft in Piraeus Great Harbour.*

December 1998, mainly due to the importance of the lifeline that the company provides to the eastern group of islands from which it operates. While the Ministry of Shipping dithered over the potential reallocation of operating licences on the route, the service just carried on and the company's problems appear to have been solved by a substantial injection of capital from ANEK, who acquired a 25% shareholding in early 1999 and DANE has since chartered its *Candia* to operate until a degree of stability is restored.

The company's principal service to Rhodes is provided by the Japanese-built *Patmos* and *Rodos*, impressive vessels with substantial capacity for passengers in cabins on the long overnight crossings, and for freight traffic on their substantial vehicle decks. The services to the smaller islands in the chain are provided by the *Candia* and the *Ialyssos*, built in 1966 as the *Finnpartner* for service in the Baltic. Not a popular ship with her passengers, and with her appearance marred by the addition of sponsons which have helped to address her disturbing habit of rolling in the strong north-easterly winds of the Aegean, her former running mate, the *Kamiros* was replaced in 1996 and now sails in the Adriatic. Her replacement, the *Leros* provided an efficient if not particularly elegant replacement until her destruction by fire in December 1998. She is now laid-up at Elefsis and surely cannot be revived again.

DD Ferries

A recent arrival in the trade to Evia, this company operates the single and unlovely vessel *Express Karistos* several times daily from Rafina to Marmari in southern Evia. She was built in Greece and after initial service as the *Aetos*, subsequently operated with Agapitos as their *Dodekanissos*. Inadequate in size and accommodation for their further requirements, she spent many years as the *Corfu Sea*, operating an erratic timetable between that island and Igoumenitsa before entering service in the Aegean.

Dodecanese Hydrofoils

One of several companies appearing to have its origins in the Ilio operation, Dodecanese Hydrofoils operate seven Russian-built craft on routes between Patmos, Leros, Kos and Rhodes, with diversions to other, smaller islands in the chain. They provide a regular and reliable service, but with the usual assault on travellers' ears from their throbbing engines whose design originated in Soviet tank technology. There is nothing remarkable about the craft, although their white livery with blue and red trim do provide an elegant finish to a type of vessel which is commonplace in the Aegean.

Euboea Shipping

The transliteration of Greek names into English is notoriously difficult, and the island more generally known as Evia is also sometimes presented as Euboea. This company does not, however, serve the island whose name it carries, but rather trades from Volos to the Sporades and have chosen to name their newly-built ship, introduced in the summer of 1999, as the *Panagia Skiathou* after the main church of the island which she is principally to serve. Very much a day ferry, her passenger capacity of 1,000 in a vessel with a tonnage of only 1,500, suggests that the newness of her construction is not balanced by great luxury in the accommodation she provides.

Flying Dolphins

Numerically much the largest fleet operating in Greek waters, the Flying Dolphins were established by George Livanos, whose other shipping operations include ownership of some of the largest supertankers plying the seas of the world. Using Russian-built hydrofoils of the Kometa class (with a couple from the generally similar Kolkhida type), he accumulated a fleet of 28 of the vessels, carrying between 100 and 116 passengers on routes initially from both harbours at Piraeus to most parts of the Saronic Gulf and which steadily extended through the Cyclades in the 1980s and then along the eastern coast of the Peloponnese. It took considerable effort and patience to develop a trade using these unconventional vessels amongst the conservative travellers of the Greek islands, but the frequency and speed of the service has made up for the rough and noisy passages which they have provided. Island dwellers seem distressingly suspect to seasickness, but the remarkably large number who silently settle into the seats of these ungainly vessels is a demonstration of their confidence that, however rough the passage, it will soon be over. The atmosphere on board, which assumes that chain-smoking is a compulsory requirement of transportation, gives plenty to think about as the spray from the passing waves obliterates the view through the windows of the craft.

Not initially associated with enormous reliability, the Flying Dolphins (which used the trading name CERES) established an enviable reputation by providing a generous quantity of spare vessels to cover for breakdowns and providing an extensive and heavily used repair facility at Keratsini, between Piraeus and Perama.

In 1997 the Russian-built craft were joined by three larger vessels from the Sicilian operator Siremar, which were used to introduce new services from the Great Harbour at Piraeus to

Above: *Heavily rebuilt but still recognisable as the former Townsend* **Free Enterprise VIII** *– later P&O's* **Pride of Canterbury** *– GA Ferries'* **Romilda** *leaving Piraeus on her long service via the small islands of the southern and eastern Cyclades and Sitia in eastern Crete to Rhodes.*

the nearer islands of the Cyclades. Marketed as 'Mega-Dolphins', they provide a better class of accommodation on the upper deck while a small bar is provided below.

The only modern vessel in the fleet until recently was the *Flying Cat 1*, a Fjellstrand Flying Cat constructed in Norway in 1990 for the company and employed on the principal commuter services between Piraeus and Hydra. A conventional example of a 40-metre class more commonly to be found in the cold waters of the Norwegian fjords, she seems curiously out of place in the baking atmosphere of an Athens afternoon but is greatly appreciated by her regular passengers.

In 1998 the admirable *Flying Dolphin 2000* joined the fleet – a passenger-only craft from the Austal Shipyard in Western Australia. Her 516 passenger capacity is more than four times as great as the Russian-built craft that she runs alongside on the route from the Great Harbour at Piraeus to Aegina. Appearing rather larger than the service demands, she has proved a worthwhile application of effort by her Australian builders, who have since been awarded an order for three new car-carrying catamarans, more typical of Austal vessels used elsewhere in Europe, the largest being a 92-metre vessel to be introduced onto a new route between Piraeus, Sifnos in the western Cyclades, and Santorini in the southern Cyclades in the year 2000. The other pair are 72-metre vessels for services from Volos and Thessalonika to Chios and Lesbos and to take over Minoan's operations in the central Cyclades previously sailed by their *High Speed I*. The licensing of these new routes has provoked considerable controversy among the existing operators and intense competition will no doubt result.

In late 1998 the Flying Dolphins operation was merged into a new joint venture between the Livanos family and Minoan Lines which now trade as Minoan Flying Dolphins. The new company, which uses the style C&M (CERES and Minoan), has announced the intention to launch itself onto the Athens stock market in late 1999/early 2000 to provide the capital required for the newbuildings proposed above, and the resulting changes in the company's profile have further

improved upon the excellent reputation of the company during its earlier period under the control of the Livanos family.

GA Ferries

Another manifestation of the Agoudimos family, GA Ferries have not been frightened to experiment with vessels and routes during their short history. After operation in the early 1990s in the Adriatic, they have become an exclusively Aegean operator in more recent times, and now provide many of the principal services to both the Dodecanese and the north-east Aegean islands, a long roundabout service to Rhodes via Crete and head-to-head competition with Minoan on the route between Thessalonika and Heraklion. Under the charismatic leadership of Gerassimos Agoudimos the company has a reputation among the very best of Greek ferry operators.

Four of the vessels in the current fleet are generally similar Japanese-built vessels of the early 1970s, converted and splendidly extended in shipyards in Greece in the early 1990s. The *Daliana*, *Marina*, *Milena* and *Rodanthi* all provide a similar and generally comfortable standard of accommodation on the long routes that they serve. Very much in the first class of Greek domestic ferries, their technical systems as well as hulls and engines are maintained in excellent condition.

Far more interesting is the *Romilda*, built as the last of the Townsend Car Ferries series of ships for the Dover station in 1974 as the *Free Enterprise VIII*, remaining in the Townsend Thoresen fleet until acquisition by P&O in early 1987. Subsequently renamed the *Pride of Canterbury*, she continued in service latterly on the Dover to Boulogne service until it closed at the beginning of 1993. She then joined her current operator's fleet where, somewhat rebuilt with a more conventional bow and extensions to the superstructure aft, she presents an unusual profile. She now appears to operate mainly as a subsidy-collector for her operators, running between Piraeus and Rhodes on a long route through the Cyclades, touching Crete at Sitia on the way to Rhodes. She also manages to fit in a journey around the Turkish coast through the north-eastern Aegean during the course of her fussy timetable, during which she occasionally encounters her former fleetmate the *Pride of Winchester* running with LANE to eastern Crete.

Operating on one of the longest of the routes in the Aegean, the *Dimitroula* is an example of a class of ferry built for the Italian state-owned company Tirrenia in the late 1970s and requiring only modest refitting for her new services. A comfortable and cheerfully-run vessel, her itinerary takes her from Thessalonika through the Sporades and the whole chain of the Cyclades on her thrice-weekly route to Heraklion in Crete.

Previously a fairly conventional operator, albeit with a good nose for choosing the right vessel and the courage to experiment with routes to achieve the most profitable results, GA Ferries stole a march on their competitors in 1999 by announcing the purchase of Scandlines' fast monohull *Berlin Express* to enter service after the 1999 summer. A sister of the *Jetliner* used by P&O between Cairnryan and Larne and capable of a speed of 36 knots, she represents one of the more successful of her type of vessel, albeit she has not seemed entirely comfortable on the service between Gedser in southern Denmark and Rostock in eastern Germany to which she came after only one season on the now-closed Danish route between Grenaa and Hundested. Her new name, and the route on which she was to be deployed, had not been announced at the time that this book closed for press.

Golden Ferries

The difficulties of maintaining a profitable service between the mainland and the island of Kythera are noted in Chapter 13. Following the demise of Miras Ferries, the route from Gytheion in the southern Peloponnese (close to ancient Sparta) to the island has been taken over by the new company of Golden Ferries. They operate a single vessel, *Maria-Pa* – an interesting ship, originally built in Italy for service to Malta, she provides a useful service along the very attractive coastline south of Gytheion, although her future cannot be taken for granted in the context of the collapse of various earlier operators on the route.

Above: *Typical of the ex-Japanese ferries which make up the bulk of the GA Ferries fleet, the* **Milena** *entering the port of Piraeus is seen passing the ancient column which stands within the naval dockyard.*

Above: *The large ex-Japanese* **Marina** *getting under way from Piraeus on a sailing to Kos.*

Goutos Lines

For long a rather dreary operator of short-distance vessels to Evia and Kea, Goutos Lines emerged in the second half of the 1990s as one of the principal enthusiasts of high-speed vessels in the Aegean.

Characteristic of their earlier services, the *Papadiamantis II* is a long-standing vessel in the services from Volos through the Sporades. By no means an elegant ship, her apparent lack of funnels is due to the curious way in which her superstructure has been extended upwards beyond the tops of the original funnel design, with little more than long exhaust pipes left sticking out above the perspex roof of the new upper deck. She maintains an extremely efficient service and the remarkable sound of her engines reversing as she approaches port can always be relied on to attract the attention of passers-by.

During the 1970s and '80s, the services to the island of Kea from the mainland port of Lavrion, close to the southernmost point of Attica at Cape Sounion, were provided by the remarkable *Ioulis Kea* – an extraordinary conversion from the Mersey ferry *Royal Daffodil* with most of her superstructure replaced by an enclosed box of a vehicle deck. She was replaced after the 1991 season by the *Myrina Express*, another Greek-built vessel of modest dimensions which provides a regular and comfortable service across the notorious Kea Channel.

One of the more extraordinary vessels in the Greek fleet joined the operations of Goutos Lines in 1996. The large car-carrying catamaran *Supercat Haroula* was built at Perama to provide a supposedly express service through the Cyclades from Rafina. Delivered over a year late, she presents a remarkable profile as she ploughs around the northern Cyclades. Although somewhat faster than the conventional ferries that she competes with, she appears extremely difficult to manoeuvre, and berthing in harbours can take from fifteen to thirty minutes, during which much of the speed advantage that she may have gained on passage is wasted. Her interior accommodation is, however, far better than the hideous exterior might suggest, with extensive sun decks and comfortably air-conditioned lounges. The lack of success of her design is demonstrated by the extensive advertising that her operators appear to feel the need to provide in a route where her competitors confine themselves to a few signs

Above: *The extraordinary (and not particularly fast)* **Supercat Haroula** *of Goutos Lines arriving at Rafina in 1997.*

outside the praktoreions at which their tickets sell.

However, in 1998 Goutos entered the high-speed market seriously with the acquisition of the *Athina 2004* – an FBM Tri-Cat capable of a speed of 50 knots, built at FBM in Cowes on the Isle of Wight. Taking her name from the excitement which the award of the Olympic Games in the year 2004 to Athens has inspired in at least some parts of Greek society, she is an example of the class of vessel developed for use between Hong Kong and Macau and operated there with notable success. Modified with strengthened stern transoms for making 'Mediterranean Moor' berthings and with her exhausts extended upwards to avoid broiling passengers boarding at her stern, she was renamed for the 1999 season as the *Supercat Athina*. She provoked the first serious competition with the Rafina consortium's *Sea Jet I*, although this in turn was answered by increased competition from Strintzis who took over operation of the vessel on their own and added a second similar craft to the route to Rafina to Mykonos. Goutos initially responded by acquiring a further similar vessel, originally intended for Ventouris Ferries operations from Rafina but sold to Goutos during building and then re-sold before delivery to Agapitos Lines (see above).

Hermes Hydrofoils

Originally operating from Rafina through the northern Cyclades and between Rhodes and Turkey, this company has since reduced its services although they continued to be advertised in 1998. It operates a comparatively interesting fleet, all of which have seen service in the British Isles. The *Iptamenos Hermes I* and the *Iptamenos Hermes III* were respectively the *Condor 4* and *Condor 5*, operating in services between the Channel Islands and France until being replaced by more modern tonnage in the early 1990s. The rather smaller Italian-built *Nike I* and *Nike II* were well-known for many years in Southampton Water as Red Funnel's *Shearwater 3* and *Shearwater 4* and have subsequently operated in the Dodecanese.

Hydra Lines

Operators of a single vessel, albeit probably the most comfortable en route from Piraeus to Hydra and Spetses. Modernistic in her appearance, the *Georgios 2* has a somewhat larger capacity for both vehicles and passengers than her competitors and attracts much local business as a result.

Ilio Lines

Ilio have operated hydrofoils in the Aegean for most of the last twenty years providing a few daily services to Rafina, but mainly operating within the central and northern Cyclades. With a habit of changing their schedules every year, sometimes apparently every day, their services pose particular problems to describe but the vessels are rather more predictable – further examples of the Kometa and Kolkhida class hydrofoils built in the late 1970s and early 1980s, many having seen previous service in Russia and Poland. The Company has spawned several other hydrofoil operations listed under Dodecanese Hydrofoils, Samos Hydrofoils and Speed Lines.

LANE (the Lassithi Shipping Company)

In contrast to the thrusting districts of central and western Crete, the eastern end of the Island is a largely agricultural society with the occasional resort for package tourists. It appeared an unusual place to spawn a ferry service in the 1990s, particularly in view of the excellent communications between the mainland and Heraklion, no more than 125 kilometres from the eastern tip of the Island. However, the citizens of the Lassithi county gave a further demonstration of Cretan independence of outlook when establishing their own shipping company at the end of 1994 to provide regular links between the small harbours of Sitia and Agios Nikolaos and the mainland. Undeterred by a board of directors who were all new to shipping, the company provides useful links between the island and Piraeus via Milos in the western Cyclades to the north – while continuing each weekend to the east to serve

Above: *LANE Lines'* **Vitsentzos Kornaros** *approaching Sitia in Eastern Crete on her regular service from Piraeus via the Western Cyclades. She is little altered from her earlier service with Townsend Thoresen as the* **Viking Viscount** *and later P&O as the* **Pride** *of Winchester.*

Kassos and Karpathos as one of the closest approaches the Greek ferries manage to a mini-cruise.

The successors to a series of operators who have attempted to exploit the available subsidies for running on these comparatively unpopular routes, LANE have had the good fortune to acquire the elegant Townsend Thoresen ferry *Viking Viscount* – later P&O's *Pride of Winchester*. Little altered from her days sailing from Portsmouth, even the blue 'go faster' stripe from P&O days has been preserved – she sails as the *Vitsentzos Kornaros* and she provides comfortable accommodation in a full range of cabins as well as deck accommodation but, whilst running full in the high summer, has tended to run almost empty at other seasons. Her triple engines and propellers have ensured that she has always been immensely reliable and not a single sailing was lost due to mechanical defect in her first five years in the Aegean.

In late 1998 rumours abounded (not for the first time) that LANE was to merge with Minoan and the latter company issued a series of statements which suggested that merger was inevitable. Combined with a shrewd counter-bid from ANEK, this roused the local shareholders and, whilst accepting the impossibility of continuing the service independently, they have chosen to ally themselves with the western Cretan company to lock out the sometimes arrogant citizens of Heraklion from their affairs. ANEK has responded by introducing the Japanese-built *Talos* from their Adriatic services as the *Ierapetra* to run alongside the existing vessel in a daily service intended to challenge GA Ferries with their *Romilda* on the circuitous route she runs to Rhodes. The future deployment of the vessels and the development of the services of this company give much scope for speculation, but their timings are much more sympathetic to the traveller wishing for a restful arrival in Crete than those of the other operators and the friendliness of the welcome aboard the *Vitsentzos Kornaros* encourages regular repeat business.

Lefakis

Operators of two rather different vessels on the heavily trafficked route between Piraeus and Aegina, Lefakis sail in close alliance with Hydra Lines (see above). Although their modest sized *Eftychia* has a novel appearance, rather of the nature of a private motor cruiser which grew up to provide an enclosed deck for half a dozen lorries, her fleet mate the *Saronikos* is a more extraordinary vessel. Apparently built to be a landing craft, her vehicle deck has been entirely enclosed and is surrounded by galleries linking the passenger accommodation to the bow ramp while a more extensive superstructure than normal is provided. While undoubtedly a great improvement on some vessels on the longer runs from Piraeus to Hydra, Spetses and Porto Heli, neither is able to provide the range of amenities or style of Agapitos Express Ferries' *Express Danae* with which they run in competition.

Above: *The second vessel in the fleet of Lassithi A.N.E., the* **Ierapetra** *joined the company in 1999 after previous service in the Adriatic with ANEK as their* **Talos**.

Above: *The Milos Express sailing from Piraeus in 1990.*

Lindos Lines

Another of the companies to have tried without much success to operate the services from Piraeus around the eastern Peloponnese to Kythera and western Crete, Lindos Lines is now the operator of a single ship but an exceptionally interesting one. The *Milos Express* was built in 1969 as Sealink's *Vortigern*. Designed to operate both as a train ferry between Dover and Dunkerque and as a car ferry on the then principal service from Dover to Boulogne, she subsequently became a stalwart on all of the Cross-Channel routes of the railway shipping services from Dover and Folkestone with occasional forays around the other railway ports of the United Kingdom. Her final operations were in 1987, including a spell on charter to P&O in the aftermath of the sinking of the *Herald Free Enterprise*, she became surplus during the economic downturn of the late 1980s and was sold in 1988 to her current operators.

Somewhat rebuilt at the stern with additional superstructure and new cabin accommodation, she retains the railway tracks provided originally to carry the sleeping cars of the 'Night Ferry' through train between Paris, Brussels and London. Operating entirely on the western Cyclades route to Milos via Kythnos, Serifos and Sifnos, with occasional diversions through the smaller islands in the group, she now shows her age and appears particularly vulnerable to competition which will surely arrive in the relatively near future. Sharing her service with the *Pegasus* of Ventouris Ferries, another company with less financial muscle than it once had, it may not long before she joins the growing collection of laid-up ferries at Elefsis.

Mililis Lines

After operating in the fleet of Goutos Lines (see above) for many years, the tiny *Karistos* was taken over by this company in 1996. A vessel of character rather than comfort, she has the highly unusual feature of a proper lifting bow but no other access to her car deck. She operates four times a day between Rafina and Evia, alternating between calls at Karistos and Marmari.

Minoan Lines

Undoubtedly the dominant force in the Aegean ferry market, and perhaps the best in all Greece, Minoan was established in 1972 with widespread shareholding throughout central Crete. Services commenced in May 1974 with the introduction of the *Minos* – one of a series of extraordinary conversions from tankers built in the early 1950s achieved by the yards at Perama. Capable of carrying 220 vehicles through her side door and 1,000 passengers she represented a practical way of providing an inexpensive ferry at a time when second-hand car ferries were virtually unavailable in the market place. Despite the lack of manoeuvrability given by her single propeller and her archaic appearance she remained in service until 1984 and in many ways represented the foundation of the line's success.

In 1976 the first modern vessel joined the fleet, the former *Tor Hollandia* which had been replaced on North Sea services by the admirable *Tor Britannia* and introduced new standards to island services. As the *Ariadne* she served Minoan Lines for 23 years; after displacement from the routes to Crete by the arrival of new vessels she served first in the Adriatic and then

Above: *The little Karistos was built in Greece in 1968 and is seen backing away from Rafina in a characteristic cloud of exhaust fumes as she departs for Evia.*

Above: *The first modern car ferry in Minoan Lines' fleet, the **Ariadne** leaving Piraeus in the last of her 22 seasons with the company in 1998. Little altered from her days as the **Tor Hollandia** on the North Sea, this elegant ship has now joined Fragline for further service in the Adriatic (see page 35).*

between Piraeus and the Cyclades from 1996 until sale in early 1999 to Fragline, as noted in Chapter 10. Subsequent purchases of the two Swedish Lloyd vessels which served as the *Knossos* and *Festos* until 1997 led to further development of the company – they have been replaced by new tonnage and now sail in the fleet of Diler Lines (again see Chapter 10).

Longest serving of the current fleet is the *El Greco*, introduced into service in 1981 after nine years in Japan. She maintains a comparatively conventional appearance for a ship of her origins and served on most of the company's routes before moving in 1996 to the long service operated three times weekly between Thessalonika and Heraklion via the Cyclades. A most comfortable ship on which to travel on this fascinating route, she carries considerable intermediate traffic and a prodigious quantity of freight avoiding the unpleasant drive down the National Road to Athens and the overnight passage from there.

One of the few exclusively freight ro-ros in the Greek fleet, the *Agia Galini* joined the Minoan fleet in 1986 to provide

additional freight accommodation on the main service from Piraeus to Heraklion. Although frequently mentioned as a potential disposal when new tonnage has been proposed, she continues to operate and is unlikely to leave the fleet until the introduction of new vessels in 2001 which promise to revolutionise current ferry services between Piraeus and Crete. Built in Romania, she had an itinerant career before joining the Minoan fleet in which she has a more gentle existence with thrice weekly return crossings from the capital to the island.

The current vessels on the mainline service between Piraeus and Heraklion are the *King Minos* and her close sister the *N. Kazantzakis*. Sister ships built in Japan, they joined Minoan in 1987 and 1990 respectively and, although not particularly speedy ships, provide a range of extremely comfortable accommodation and an attractive style of service. At summer weekends they provide additional daylight

Below: *One of the few pure ro-ro vessels in the Greek ferry fleets, Minoan Lines **Agia Galini** at her berth in Piraeus.*

crossings placing a considerable strain on the turnaround available at each end of their journey. They will be replaced in 2001 by the large newbuildings *Festos Palace* and the *Knossos Palace* now being constructed at Fincantieri in Italy. At 210 metres in length, some 30% longer than the existing vessels, they will have an impressive capacity of 2,200 passengers and 1,000 cars and 1,560 lane metres for vehicle accommodation. Perhaps most interestingly they have been specified to have a service speed of 29.5 knots which will enable them to operate between Piraeus and Crete in six hours, rather than the eleven hours taken by the current pair. The eventual deployment must however be subject to some further speculation and the possibility exists of the Heraklion route being worked by one of the pair whilst

Above: *Now the mainstay of the long service from Thessalonika to Heraklion in Crete, the Japanese-built El Greco was Minoan Line's first vessel in the Adriatic trade in 1981.*

the other operates to Chania on a route newly regained by Minoan in a recent round of licensing application, subject to the condition that new tonnage is introduced to the route.

Between 1997 and 1999 the company also operated the 36-knot fast craft *High Speed I* between Piraeus and Mykonos. Built in 1996 for the short-lived Adriatic operator Catamaran Ferry Lines at the Royal Schelde yard in Vlissingen, she was acquired the following year after operating an unimaginative timetable between Igoumenitsa and Brindisi. She operated twice daily to the Cyclades and proved popular with summer visitors despite her higher fares than those on conventional ferries and her lack of outside space. Very much an odd man out in the fleet, her redeployment in the Adriatic from 2000 (see Chapter 10) following closer integration in the Aegean with the fleet of Flying Dolphins will see her replaced by a new Austal catamaran of the Flying Dolphins fleet in the highly competitive trade with the Cyclades.

Although increasingly focused on the demands of the Athens Stock Exchange where 25% of its stock is now traded, Minoan remains a firmly Cretan-based company with its headquarters in Heraklion's main street. The aggressive nature of its expansion is demonstrated not only by the spate of recent orders noted here and in Chapter 10, but also by its ownership of one of Greece's largest Internet service providers, the take over in early 1999 of a majority shareholding in the independent airline Air Greece and its merger with the Flying Dolphins business described above. It is now in the big league of world ferry operators, having the

eighth largest fleet by tonnage (185,314 tons) and tenth greatest by number of ships with twelve vessels in the current fleet. Under the charismatic leadership of General Manager Panayotis Kassapakis, Minoan is now the largest transporter of passengers in Greece, even surpassing Olympic Airways. The company appears well-placed to further expand its operations in the years ahead and, unlike its competitors, does so with a fleet containing a remarkably high proportion of modern vessels.

Miras Ferries

Until it ceased operations on the route in 1997, Miras Ferries operated the interesting run between Piraeus and the eastern Peloponnese, continuing to the islands of Kythera and Antikythera and the western part of Crete. The company remains active as part of the consortium from Kilini to Zakynthos in the Adriatic (see Chapter 10) but its Aegean operations structure have ended, at least for the present.

In addition to the dumpy *Martha* which previously operated between Gytheion and Kythera, a route now taken over by Golden Ferries, the fleet contained the *Theseus*. This was an elegant conversion achieved in Perama from the former B&I freighter *Dundalk*, later Sealink's *St Cybi*. A particularly comfortable vessel in Greek service, her sudden withdrawal brought an end to this most attractive route. She has since been laid-up in the harbour at Keratsini in Piraeus, near to the container terminal.

Mykonos A.N.E.

The only other freight ro-ro serving the Aegean at present, the *Mykonos II* provide a daily freight service between Rafina and the island of Mykonos. Typical of the early generation of roll-on roll-off freighters, she saw early service in the North Sea as the *Ro-Ro Anglia* before a series of charters and finally sale to her current operator.

NEL (the Maritime Company of Lesbos)

Despite enjoying a virtual monopoly in recent years in services between the mainland and the North-East Aegean islands of Chios and Lesbos, NEL Lines have provided efficient and comfortable services with a very varied fleet. Smartly turned out and conveniently timed, the five vessels have provided an admirable network between Piraeus, Rafina, Thessalonika and the island ports. Pressure from other

Above: *The N. Kazantzakis sailing from Piraeus for Heraklion in Crete on an additional morning sailing in the high summer of 1994.*

Above: *Two British car ferries of the 1960s of very different styles. Originally Ellerman Wilson's* **Spero** *and Townsend's* **Free Enterprise** *but seen at Piraeus in 1990 as NEL Lines* **Sappho** *and Ventouris Sea Lines'* **Kimolos**.

operators combined with political interference have seen the awarding of a new license to operate to Lesbos to Strintzis, as noted below. The same exercise has, however, seen a new licence awarded to NEL to operate between Lesbos, the Sporades and northern Greece offering scope for an expansion in the company's current business. Whether the current excellent service will be maintained in a more competitive environment must remain a matter of conjecture at present. Previously successfully traded on the Athens Stock Exchange, a new issue of shares amounting to 20% of the company was taken in late 1998 by ANEK as part of its strategy of expanding its ownership of companies in the Greek domestic market.

Oldest and spectacularly ugliest of the vessels in the fleet, the *Agios Rafael* is a freighter on which modest and rather spindly looking passenger accommodation has been added. Taking her turn with the less popular sailings, she does provide admirable freight space on her vehicle deck.

Among the earlier vessels of Viking Line built to operate through the icy Baltic seas, the first *Mariella* of 1970 joined the fleet of NEL in 1981 as the *Alcaeos*. A product of the Tito Brod yard in the then Yugoslavia, she has now been largely supplanted by larger tonnage but operates an unusual service between Rafina, the north-east Aegean Islands and the northern mainland port of Kavala.

Perhaps most interesting of the vessels in the current fleet, the *Sappho* was built in 1966 as Ellerman Wilson's *Spero* to run between Hull

and Gothenburg. Never successful with an operator which was attempting the painful transition from conventional break-bulk cargo vessels in an era of industrial unrest, she was tried in 1972 on a service to Zeebrugge before withdrawal in 1973 and sale to Greece. Comparatively little altered externally, she provides comfortable accommodation for 1,430 passengers, or at least for the 480 of them who can be accommodated in the cabins that she offers.

The regular choices for the busiest sailings on the company are the *Mytilene* and the *Theofilos*. The former was built in Japan and elegantly converted to her current role while the later was built as TT Line's third *Nils Holgersson* – a sister

Above: *Her profile little altered from her service with Ellerman's Wilson Lines'* **Spero**, *NEL Lines'* **Sappho** *at speed in the Saronic Gulf on passage from Lesbos to Piraeus.*

of the current *Fedra* of Minoan Lines. Her subsequent career was somewhat different, including a spell of operating between Melbourne and Tasmania as the *Abel Tasman* until replaced by a ship from the next generation of TT Line and sale to Ventouris Ferries, who owned her for a short period under the name *Pollux*. During her career she has acquired ugly additional accommodation blocks at her stern and on top of her superstructure but although she now lacks the elegance of her sister in the Minoan Fleet, she is able to provide accommodation for a large quantity of passengers in at least relatively comfortable cabins on her long crossings.

In 1999 the fleet was augmented by the former *Euromantique* – built as a ro-ro to operate in Australia between Sydney and Tasmania under the name *Union Hobart*, she was subsequently sold to A.K. Ventouris and operated with them as the *Agia Methodia* and later chartered by them in 1994 to the Eurolink operation which replaced the far more luxurious services of Olau Line between Sheerness and Vlissingen. A relatively comfortable ship, despite her modest sized accommodation, she is better equipped to operate in the Aegean than the southern North Sea and provides an interesting extension to the varied fleet of NEL. She carries the somewhat unexpected name of *Taxiarches* during the current charter – at least an improvement on her last name.

However, the greatest change to the company's operations is scheduled for 2000 when the fast monohull *Aeolos* will join the fleet from the Saint Nazaire yard of Alsthom Leroux. Operating at a speed of 36 knots she should be able to bring the port of Mytilene within six hours of Piraeus and the success that has been made by the similar vessels operating for SNCM suggests that she will help to enhance the reputation of this excellent company as it faces the forthcoming onset of competition.

Nomicos Lines

Operating a fleet of four modest sized vessels, principally in the Sporades, this long - established operator is unusual in the Aegean in equipping its ships with a grey hull and funnels carrying a white cross of St Andrew a blue background – a considerable contrast to the white hulls and more trendy funnel designs of other operators. The most elegant in the fleet is the Greek-built *Lemnos* 1976; the *Skopelos* of 1965 saw initial service in Sweden while the *Macedon* and the *Anemos* are Japanese-built vessels of 1972 and 1975 respectively. Well-run on routes sailing out of Volos and Thessalonika as well as Piraeus, the only competition that they face at present comes from the rather less imposing *Papadiamantis II* of Goutos Lines – and the inevitable hydrofoils. The award of the new service to NEL to connect Lesbos with the mainland via the Sporades will however add new competition to the Nomicos operations.

Paraskevas

Operators of the only Westamarin catamaran of her class in the Aegean, Paraskevas are another of the companies competing in the trade between Piraeus and Aegina. The 1972 built *Keravnos* is an example of the W86 catamaran found in many parts of Scandinavia and the Channel Islands. She now appears extremely dated compared to the newer craft operating on the route but has a loyal following among the commuters from the island.

Salamis

The unlovely commercial and residential island of Salamis is briefly described in Chapter 13. Vehicular traffic is concentrated on the short crossing from Perama to the island

Above: *Seen as she leaves Piraeus on main line of NEL to Lesbos, the **Mytilene** was heavily rebuilt after Japanese service as the **Vega**.*

capital of Salamina with about twenty landing craft ferries in use at the amazingly busy peak hours but only three or four suffice during the middle of the day. Passenger services by-pass the congestion on the road between Athens and Perama by leaving from the heart of the Great Harbour at Piraeus. Once served by the ubiquitous Russian hydrofoils, the service is now back in the hands of a small fleet of simple wooden passenger vessels.

Samos Hydrofoils

Another spin-off from the Ilio business, this company operates to Kometa-type hydrofoils on routes from the island of Samos to Patmos and Kos in the Dodecanese. More remarkably, a weekly route is operated to Alexandroupolis in the far north-eastern corner of the mainland from Samos taking twelve hours to reach its destination. No doubt an important strategic link, the effect of a journey of that duration in such a noisy and bouncy vessel is better imagined than experienced.

Saronic Poseidon

The operating name of a consortium of operators providing ten landing craft ferries which operate the hourly service from the Great Harbour in Piraeus to the island of Aegina. Like the similar operation to Corfu reviewed in Chapter 10, they operate fleet of generally elderly and noisy landing craft in competition from newer and faster vessels, the inherent simplicity and economy of the ships of this sort and the ability of the consortium to provide a very regular and reliable service means that they remain the dominant operator for vehicular traffic. In 1999 the consortium finally introduced the *Poseidon Hellas* to its services. Not vastly different from the other vessels in the operation she has the unusual distinction of having been laid down seventeen years before introduction into service. The vessels exchange timetables and lay-by periods daily so as to share in a most satisfactory manner the available trade and to avoid imposing too great a strain on the vessels or their crews. A roundtrip to Aegina on these vessels, chugging out through the Great Harbour of Piraeus and the extensive anchorages that occupy most of the 25-kilometre passage to the island can make a pleasant excursion on a summer afternoon.

Sea Falcon Lines

Yet another operator of fast craft in the highly competitive trade between Piraeus and Aegina, Sea Falcon operate four examples of the Russian-built Meteor class of hydrofoil making no pretence at a regular interval service, they concentrate on the rush hour trade in which they appear to have been reasonably successful.

Speed Lines

Another derivative from the Ilio business, Speed Lines operate two more Russian-built hydrofoils, one a Kometa and the other a Kolkhida named *Ios Dolphin* and *Santorini Dolphin* respectively on services around the central Cyclades.

Strintzis Lines

A long-standing family-controlled company whose first vessel was acquired in 1897, Strintzis has emerged from a period in mid-1990s when it seemed to be very much in the shadow of other companies to a resurgence under the chairmanship of Gerassimos Strintzis as one of the dominant players in the ferry market.

After establishing themselves in the ferry business in the Adriatic, the company moved into the Aegean when they transferred the *Eptanisos* and the *Delos* to run out of Rafina through the northern and central Cyclades in the late 1980s. The former Newhaven-Dieppe twins established a reputation for reliability and comfort of service, although a change in the priorities of the company saw the *Delos* return to the Adriatic for a final spell of service operating out of Kilini. The acquisition in 1992 of the former Japanese ferry *Izu Maru 3*, renamed as the *Superferry*, led to an expansion in capacity which was continued in the following year. The former RMT *Prince Laurent* was introduced into the Rafina service as the *Superferry II* in succession to the first *Superferry* which was sent on charter to Swansea-Cork Ferries with whom she continued to operate until 1999. The Belgian vessel replaced the *Eptanisos* which followed her sister back to Kilini and the Strintzis operation in the Aegean settled with the large *Superferry II* as their biggest and smartest ship.

Extensively rebuilt, her superstructure, funnel and bow

Above: *Typical of the landing craft used on the service to Aegina, the* **Ioannis II** *leaves the Great Harbour of Piraeus as larger vessels on the longer distance ferry services load on adjoining berths.*

were renewed leaving only a few of the distinguishing side windows and her original bridge structure to remind travellers of her earlier service. While not exactly a handsome vessel, she is well equipped on board and carries a significant passenger load – her certificate is for 2,380. In 1998 she was joined by the *Ionian Sun* which appeared to run in competition with her and the other vessels of the consortium (but with all of the proceeds going to Strintzis rather than to be shared among the consortium members). This operation ceased with the return of the *Ionian Sun* to Kilini, but capacity lost was made good by the introduction of fast craft out of Rafina. The *Seajet 1* is a Westamarin 4200 catamaran built in Sweden to operate on the services in the northern Cyclades. In the winter of 1998 she was taken over from the consortium by Strintzis who have also transferred the similar *Mirage* after one season operating out of Piraeus to Aegina and renamed her the *Seajet 2*. She now operates a long route from Rafin through the Cyclades to Santorini with calls at the major islands en route.

Strintzis operations out of Piraeus have tended to be brief and have appeared unsatisfactory. In the mid-1990s they operated the *Ionian Sea* from Piraeus to the Cyclades but gave up in 1994 after which the vessel was sold to GA Ferries to sail as their *Dimitra* and was subsequently sold on to DANE with whom she sailed as the *Leros* until her destruction by fire in late 1998. The brief and apparently unsuccessful service of the *Mirage* is mentioned above.

Two ships now on order for the Aegean have the distinction of being the first conventional ships (as opposed to landing craft or fast craft) to be built in Greek shipyards for over two decades. Ordered from the Hellenic Shipyards at Skaramanga, part of the town of Elefsis (whose name was appropriated by Ian Fleming while working at the British Embassy in Athens for use as one of James Bond's arch-enemies), the purchases are being made with loans from the Greek banks which also own the yard. The *Superferry Mykonos* will join operations from Rafina in May 2001 to run via the northern Cyclades to Ikaria and Samos using her 27-knot speed to reach the distant island in no more than seven hours, in contrast to the ten hours required by the earlier generation of ferries sailing from Piraeus.

Strintzis also plan a return to Piraeus with the awarding of a new licence to operate a service to Chios and Lesbos in competition with NEL Lines using their other new ship, the *Superferry Chios* also due to be delivered in 2001 by Hellenic

Above: *During the 1998 season, Strintzis lines operated the* **Mirage** *out of Piraeus on a short-lived service to Aegina. She is seen leaving Piraeus with the cathedral behind. She now operates from Rafina to the Cyclades as the* **Seajet 2**.

Above: *The one time **Prince Laurent** of 1974 was extensively rebuilt after purchase by Strintzis Lines as their **Superferry II**. She sails in opposition to her sister ship the **Express Athina** between Rafina and Mykonos.*

Shipyards. With the 27-knot speed that has become standard for Strintzis newbuildings she promises to introduce serious competition into a business which has appeared very stable for many years.

Strintzis is in an expansionist and competitive phase at the end of the twentieth century and the apparently easy availability of further capital from the Athens Stock Exchange makes the ordering of further vessels for the Aegean highly probable. Their distinctive blue-hulled livery and impressive accommodation make Strintzis vessels among the most attractive vessels in the seas of Greece.

Superfast Ferries

As noted in Chapter 10, the expansionist management of this thriving company has repeatedly attempted to introduce services in the Aegean, but political interference has regularly prevented it from doing so – most recently when its application to operate to Crete was turned down in favour of the existing operators in 1998. With six vessels now on order at HDW in Kiel and options for further expansions of the fleet it is to be expected that the company will shortly secure the right to operate the Aegean either by taking over an existing operator or by obtaining new licences. If it does, it can be expected that it will have a similar effect to that already seen in the Adriatic of driving out of business the older and less financially secure businesses from its target market.

Right: *Loading for her regular evening sailing to the nearer Cyclades, the **Georgios Express** was altered only by a simple extension to her stern superstructure from her days as RTM's **Roi Baudouin**.*

Thassos A.N.E.

Operating in the far north-eastern corner of the Greek Aegean, the Thassos Shipping Company operate five landing craft ferries and a Russian-built Kometa hydrofoil on services between Kavala and the island of Thassos.

Ventouris Ferries

Through the 1980s and early 1990s the five Ventouris brothers established the dominant dynasty in Greek ferry shipping of the time. Their relations with one another appear to have left much to be desired with regular disputes and reports of violent incidents but by 1994 twenty-one ships were sailing with the Ventouris family name on their sides, the largest division being that of Ventouris Ferries controlled by

Above: *The final Ventouris vessel in operation in the Aegean, the Pegasus was originally built as Adriatica's Espresso Venezia. She is seen here in 1994 during the brief period she sailed on Ventouris Ferries' Adriatic routes.*

George Ventouris. In addition to extensive services in the Adriatic, his company operated the *Bari Express* out of Rafina while brothers Antonis and Vangelis operated from Piraeus to the Saronic Gulf and Cyclades under the names of Ventouris Lines and Ventouris Sea Lines respectively. In 1995 and 1996 these Piraeus-based companies were torn apart by financial problems and loss of confidence among the banks that had provided finance to them leading to withdrawal of their ships which spent the summer of 1996 laid-up. However, Ventouris Ferries were unaffected by these problems and in order to partially fill the vacuum and, either to assist his brothers in their problems or profit from their misfortunes according to the conflicting accounts published at the time, George sent the *Pegasus* from the Adriatic to run on the western Cyclades service from Piraeus to Milos via Kythnos, Serifos and Sifnos. An elegant vessel, originally built as Adriatica's *Espresso Venezia*, she operates a complicated and frequently changing itinerary on the route in her classic white livery.

The Rafina operations with the *Bari Express* continued unchanged until the end of the 1998 season when, as noted above, the consortium of operators reverted to competing with one and other and at the same time Ventouris Ferries sold the vessel and her operating licence to Agapitos Express Ferries.

Ventouris Sea Lines

The unhappy story of the collapse of Ventouris Sea Lines is described above, but while most of the vessels in the fleet have now found new operators, the elegant *Georgios Express* remains under arrest at the northern side of the Great Harbour in Piraeus. Built in 1965 as Belgian Marine's *Roi Baudouin* she came to Greece in 1983 and operated very effectively until the collapse of her owners. Four years after her last overhaul she remains a trim and apparently well-maintained vessel and a return to service may yet occur.

Viae

Another operator to enter the trade to Kythera following the withdrawal of Miras Ferries, Viae Shipping operates their single vessel, the *Nissos Cythera* on the short route between Neapolis near to the south-eastern point of the Peloponnese at Cape Malea and the island whose name she carries. A Greek-built vessel of no particular charm, her schedules include a weekly visit to Kastelli Kissamou in western Crete.

Other Operators

Although the necessity for operating licences restricts the opportunity for new operators to enter the Aegean services, in contrast to the free enterprise noted in the Adriatic in Chapter 10, there are many smaller operators not specifically described here. Perhaps operating no more than an ancient wooden-hulled vessel between the less populous islands, they add to the fascination of this immensely varied sector of the Greek ferry scene.

Above: *The Espresso Venezia displaying her elegant original livery and classic lines.*

Part 4 - Cruises and other Ferries

Cruises by Ferry

The enormous range of cruises operating in Greek waters provide considerable material for a book of their own but are generally outside the scope of this one. Many of the ferry services reviewed within it make attractive cruises in their own right, but there are a number of opportunities to travel by a former ferry ship on a cruise which has no transport function and so lie outside the operations and routes described above.

Corfu

For many years it was possible to travel on day excursions from Piraeus on the former MacBrayne's steamer *Claymore* of 1955 sailing under the name of *City of Hydra* in partnership with *City of Piraeus* – the former Clyde vessel *Maid of Argyll*. Both operated on day cruises from the mainland to the islands of Hydra, Aegina and Poros in the Saronic Gulf. These operations have more recently taken over by newer vessels but the 'Maid' has sailed on, while the West Highland ship has retired to lay up at Elefsis.

A product of the A&J Inglis yard at Pointhouse, from which so many Clyde ferries have come, she served in Scotland for 21 years before sale in March 1974 to K Lines who have traded as Cycladic Cruises for many years but who gave up their operations in the Saronic Gulf in 1994. The *City of Piraeus* then moved westwards to the Adriatic and took up her current operation with Aronis Corfu Cruises in the one-day cruise market between the islands of Corfu and Paxos and the mainland resort of Parga. The *Maid of Argyll* sailed as the *City of Corfu* on a daily schedule leaving her home port at nine in the morning and returning some ten hours later after allowing time for swimming and shopping at her two ports of call. A lively crowd of holiday makers on these excursions appear generally taken by the ugly modernistic additions that have been made since the ship left the Clyde and unconcerned by the dubious silencing of her ageing engines.

Damaged by relatively minor groundings and a fire, she has not sailed since 1998 but it is hoped that this intriguing example of Scottish shipbuilding will remain in service for some years yet. It may be noted that her three sisters all remain afloat, one as a restaurant ship on the Thames and two converted to car ferries operating to the Isle of Capri from Naples and Sorrento.

Crete

There is a flourishing day excursion market between Crete and the extraordinary volcanic island of Santorini. Extensively marketed on Crete, and particularly popular as an optional excursion for package tour holiday makers, the long day excursion is in the hands of three companies. Minoan Cruises (a subsidiary of Minoan Lines) operate the two smartest vessels in the trade in which they are joined by Saronic Cruises *Kallish* and the hideous *Vergina Sky* of Vergina Cruise Line. Each vessel operates most frequently from Heraklion, but also includes within its weekly schedule at least one voyage from both

Rethimnon and Ayios Nikolaos. From whichever port departure is made, the sailing will be at around eight o'clock with a three and a half to four hour crossing to the volcanic island gives an arrival at lunch time at the island's southern port of Athinios. The afternoon is spent on the island before departure from the old port of Thira, 587 awkward steps below the main town, providing much trade for the muleteers and the cable way which transport visitors at considerable expense down the sheer cliff face. An early evening departure is followed by a meal to the accompaniment of Bouzoki music and Greek dancing and a not entirely sober return to Crete after dark. If the company is not too boisterous it makes a memorable and spectacular day excursion from Crete.

Perhaps the most interesting of the vessels in the trade is Minoan Cruises *Artemis*, built in 1960 as the Zeeland Steamship Company's *Koningin Wilhelmina* for the Harwich to

Above: *Minoan Cruise Line's **Artemis** at anchor in the Bay of Thera with her running mate **Minoan Prince** at the harbour beyond on cruises from Crete to the volcanic island of Santorini.*

Below: *Originally Townsend's first **Free Enterprise**, the **Kallisti** of Saronic Cruises at her berth in Heraklion in Crete prior to her daily cruise to Santorini.*

Right: *Displaying the unique DFDS side loading system at Piraeus, Louis Cruise Lines* **Princesa Kypria** *also demonstrates the extraordinary funnel added during her service with the Danish company when the aft superstructure was enlarged.*

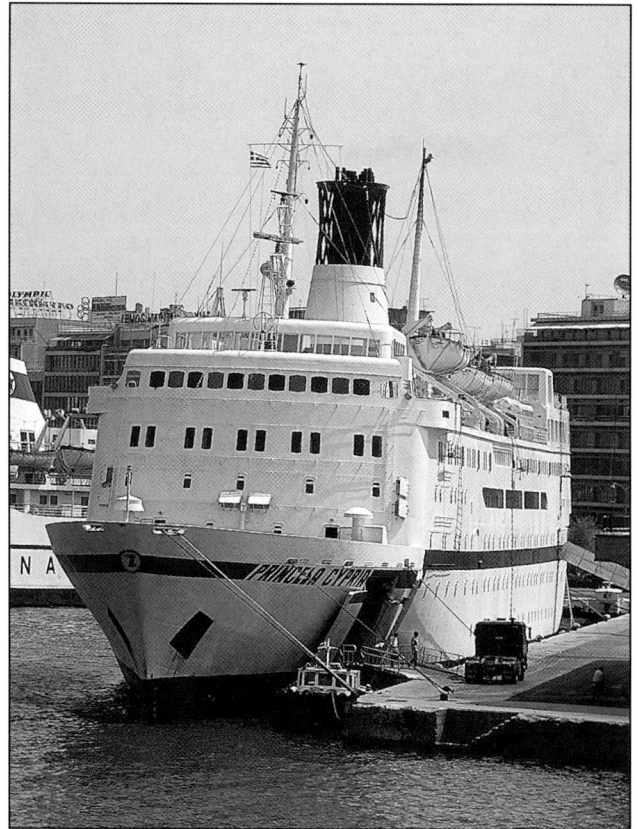

Hook of Holland day service. A futuristic looking ship when launched in 1959 with a distinctive short streamlined funnel, she was rapidly outdated by the introduction of roll-on roll-off car ferries to her route in 1968, but she continued to be used in a supporting capacity until final withdrawal in 1978. Initially purchased by Ventouris Sea Lines and operated as *Captain Constantinos* on the central Cyclades route from Piraeus to Syros, Tinos and Mykonos, she was renamed in 1981 as *Panagia Tinou* and remained as the last conventional ferry in the year-round island trades, albeit with capacity for fifty cars driven through a side ramp into a garage of notably limited height. Replaced by the former Belgian *Prins Philippe* in 1994, she spent a period in lay up before Ventouris transferred her to the day cruise market from Crete. With the collapse of her operators in 1996, she was somewhat unexpectedly taken over by Minoan Lines as part of their drive for control of the Cretan trade. Smartly refitted and equipped with a stern ramp for loading foot passengers at the very limited quay at Thira, she has remained the fastest vessel in this seasonal trade. Her continued operation despite comfortably exceeding the theoretical age limit of thirty-five years for a Greek registered passenger ship can be attributed to her regular refitting – as well as the flexible interpretation which Greek inspectors can apply to regulations.

Her running mate, the *Minoan Prince*, was built in 1973 in Japan as the ferry *Wakashio Maru* before coming to Greece in 1992. Again elegantly turned out, she operates similar cruises over a slightly longer season than the Dutch ship and equals her extensive deck space in which her passengers can enjoy the Aegean sunshine.

Another former member of the Ventouris Sea Lines fleet, the *Kallisti* has sailed in Greece for longer than in her ground-breaking role with Townsend Car Ferries as their first *Free Enterprise* ship. Entering service from Dover in 1962 and providing the first serious competition to the railway car ferries, she was rapidly outdated by the advent of drive-through ferries but remained in service until replaced by the *Spirit of Free Enterprise*, making her last sailing on Christmas Eve 1979. Entering service the following summer with Ventouris as their *Kimolos* on the Western Cyclades service, her accommodation was extended both fore and aft of the earlier superstructure but remained unmistakable as a former Townsend ship. After an unfortunate and heavily publicised grounding in 1992 she re-emerged for the following season as *Ergina* and changed her name again in 1994 to *Methodia II* for the final season with Ventouris. Already in her thirty-forth year she was not an obvious candidate for further service after the collapse of her operator, spending the 1996 season laid-up at the outer mole at Piraeus. However, she re-emerged in an all-white livery with green funnels in 1997 for Saronic Cruises operating a similar timetable to those of Minoan Cruises and otherwise little altered. She still retains her car deck and, despite her age, may yet resume ferry service in the future.

The fourth and by far the ugliest of the vessels in the day-excursion cruise market from Crete is the *Vergina Sky*, built in Japan in 1971 and brought to Greece in 1992. Her operators are Vergina Cruise Lines and she also operates a similar

timetable, although she does not appear to stray from Heraklion as her departure port. She does nothing to add grace to the islands that she serves.

Eastern Mediterranean

The Cypriot-based Louis Cruise Lines operate three intriguing ships on a service which is on the border between a ferry service and a cruise, although marketed as the latter. The vessels are based in Limassol in Cyprus and alternate calls at Piraeus with visits to Port Said and Ashdod in Egypt and Haifa in Israel.

The oldest vessel in their fleet, and in many ways the most extraordinary survivor, is the 1957 built *Princesa Amorosa* – built for Coast Lines as the *Scottish Coast*. The last Cross-Channel passenger ship for Coast Lines, she was rapidly outdated by the introduction of vehicle ferries and the closure of the overnight services between Glasgow and Belfast or Dublin. She left British waters as long ago as 1969 and served in Greece initially with Kavounides Cruises as their *Galaxias* before being reduced to a floating hotel in Vancouver in 1986. Recovered in 1989 by her current operators and refitted, she has since operated regularly and elegantly in a trade on which there is little competition but which has enabled a niche to be preserved for this intriguing survivor long after the demise of her former fleet mates.

Louis Lines turned to China in 1988 to acquire the *Lu Jiang*, a name under which she had sailed for five years after withdrawal from the DFDS fleet. One of a pair of sisters built in Italy in 1968 for the capital cities route between Copenhagen and Oslo as the *Prinsesse Margrethe* she employed the interesting side loading system for her vehicle deck which DFDS first introduced with the *England* in 1964. Although a clever way of providing vehicle ferries in an era where the infrastructure of linkspans had yet to reach many ports, the waste of space and inherent lack of freight capacity that this produced rendered her and her sister ship *Kong Olav*

Right: *Displaying the unique DFDS side loading system at Piraeus, Louis Cruise Lines* **Princesa Kypria** *also demonstrates the extraordinary funnel added during her service with the Danish company when the aft superstructure was enlarged.*

Hook of Holland day service. A futuristic looking ship when launched in 1959 with a distinctive short streamlined funnel, she was rapidly outdated by the introduction of roll-on roll-off car ferries to her route in 1968, but she continued to be used in a supporting capacity until final withdrawal in 1978. Initially purchased by Ventouris Sea Lines and operated as *Captain Constantinos* on the central Cyclades route from Piraeus to Syros, Tinos and Mykonos, she was renamed in 1981 as *Panagia Tinou* and remained as the last conventional ferry in the year-round island trades, albeit with capacity for fifty cars driven through a side ramp into a garage of notably limited height. Replaced by the former Belgian *Prins Philippe* in 1994, she spent a period in lay up before Ventouris transferred her to the day cruise market from Crete. With the collapse of her operators in 1996, she was somewhat unexpectedly taken over by Minoan Lines as part of their drive for control of the Cretan trade. Smartly refitted and equipped with a stern ramp for loading foot passengers at the very limited quay at Thira, she has remained the fastest vessel in this seasonal trade. Her continued operation despite comfortably exceeding the theoretical age limit of thirty-five years for a Greek registered passenger ship can be attributed to her regular refitting – as well as the flexible interpretation which Greek inspectors can apply to regulations.

Her running mate, the *Minoan Prince*, was built in 1973 in Japan as the ferry *Wakashio Maru* before coming to Greece in 1992. Again elegantly turned out, she operates similar cruises over a slightly longer season than the Dutch ship and equals her extensive deck space in which her passengers can enjoy the Aegean sunshine.

Another former member of the Ventouris Sea Lines fleet, the *Kallisti* has sailed in Greece for longer than in her ground-breaking role with Townsend Car Ferries as their first *Free Enterprise* ship. Entering service from Dover in 1962 and providing the first serious competition to the railway car ferries, she was rapidly outdated by the advent of drive-through ferries but remained in service until replaced by the *Spirit of Free Enterprise,* making her last sailing on Christmas Eve 1979. Entering service the following summer with Ventouris as their *Kimolos* on the Western Cyclades service, her accommodation was extended both fore and aft of the earlier superstructure but remained unmistakable as a former Townsend ship. After an unfortunate and heavily publicised grounding in 1992 she re-emerged for the following season as *Ergina* and changed her name again in 1994 to *Methodia II* for the final season with Ventouris. Already in her thirty-forth year she was not an obvious candidate for further service after the collapse of her operator, spending the 1996 season laid-up at the outer mole at Piraeus. However, she re-emerged in an all-white livery with green funnels in 1997 for Saronic Cruises operating a similar timetable to those of Minoan Cruises and otherwise little altered. She still retains her car deck and, despite her age, may yet resume ferry service in the future.

The fourth and by far the ugliest of the vessels in the day-excursion cruise market from Crete is the *Vergina Sky*, built in Japan in 1971 and brought to Greece in 1992. Her operators are Vergina Cruise Lines and she also operates a similar timetable, although she does not appear to stray from Heraklion as her departure port. She does nothing to add grace to the islands that she serves.

Eastern Mediterranean

The Cypriot-based Louis Cruise Lines operate three intriguing ships on a service which is on the border between a ferry service and a cruise, although marketed as the latter. The vessels are based in Limassol in Cyprus and alternate calls at Piraeus with visits to Port Said and Ashdod in Egypt and Haifa in Israel.

The oldest vessel in their fleet, and in many ways the most extraordinary survivor, is the 1957 built *Princesa Amorosa* – built for Coast Lines as the *Scottish Coast*. The last Cross-Channel passenger ship for Coast Lines, she was rapidly outdated by the introduction of vehicle ferries and the closure of the overnight services between Glasgow and Belfast or Dublin. She left British waters as long ago as 1969 and served in Greece initially with Kavounides Cruises as their *Galaxias* before being reduced to a floating hotel in Vancouver in 1986. Recovered in 1989 by her current operators and refitted, she has since operated regularly and elegantly in a trade on which there is little competition but which has enabled a niche to be preserved for this intriguing survivor long after the demise of her former fleet mates.

Louis Lines turned to China in 1988 to acquire the *Lu Jiang*, a name under which she had sailed for five years after withdrawal from the DFDS fleet. One of a pair of sisters built in Italy in 1968 for the capital cities route between Copenhagen and Oslo as the *Prinsesse Margrethe* she employed the interesting side loading system for her vehicle deck which DFDS first introduced with the *England* in 1964. Although a clever way of providing vehicle ferries in an era where the infrastructure of linkspans had yet to reach many ports, the waste of space and inherent lack of freight capacity that this produced rendered her and her sister ship *Kong Olav*

Part 4 - Cruises and other Ferries
Cruises by Ferry

The enormous range of cruises operating in Greek waters provide considerable material for a book of their own but are generally outside the scope of this one. Many of the ferry services reviewed within it make attractive cruises in their own right, but there are a number of opportunities to travel by a former ferry ship on a cruise which has no transport function and so lie outside the operations and routes described above.

Corfu

For many years it was possible to travel on day excursions from Piraeus on the former MacBrayne's steamer *Claymore* of 1955 sailing under the name of *City of Hydra* in partnership with *City of Piraeus* – the former Clyde vessel *Maid of Argyll*. Both operated on day cruises from the mainland to the islands of Hydra, Aegina and Poros in the Saronic Gulf. These operations have more recently taken over by newer vessels but the 'Maid' has sailed on, while the West Highland ship has retired to lay up at Elefsis.

A product of the A&J Inglis yard at Pointhouse, from which so many Clyde ferries have come, she served in Scotland for 21 years before sale in March 1974 to K Lines who have traded as Cycladic Cruises for many years but who gave up their operations in the Saronic Gulf in 1994. The *City of Piraeus* then moved westwards to the Adriatic and took up her current operation with Aronis Corfu Cruises in the one-day cruise market between the islands of Corfu and Paxos and the mainland resort of Parga. The *Maid of Argyll* sailed as the *City of Corfu* on a daily schedule leaving her home port at nine in the morning and returning some ten hours later after allowing time for swimming and shopping at her two ports of call. A lively crowd of holiday makers on these excursions appear generally taken by the ugly modernistic additions that have been made since the ship left the Clyde and unconcerned by the dubious silencing of her ageing engines.

Damaged by relatively minor groundings and a fire, she has not sailed since 1998 but it is hoped that this intriguing example of Scottish shipbuilding will remain in service for some years yet. It may be noted that her three sisters all remain afloat, one as a restaurant ship on the Thames and two converted to car ferries operating to the Isle of Capri from Naples and Sorrento.

Crete

There is a flourishing day excursion market between Crete and the extraordinary volcanic island of Santorini. Extensively marketed on Crete, and particularly popular as an optional excursion for package tour holiday makers, the long day excursion is in the hands of three companies. Minoan Cruises (a subsidiary of Minoan Lines) operate the two smartest vessels in the trade in which they are joined by Saronic Cruises *Kallish* and the hideous *Vergina Sky* of Vergina Cruise Line. Each vessel operates most frequently from Heraklion, but also includes within its weekly schedule at least one voyage from both

Rethimnon and Ayios Nikolaos. From whichever port departure is made, the sailing will be at around eight o'clock with a three and a half to four hour crossing to the volcanic island gives an arrival at lunch time at the island's southern port of Athinios. The afternoon is spent on the island before departure from the old port of Thira, 587 awkward steps below the main town, providing much trade for the muleteers and the cable way which transport visitors at considerable expense down the sheer cliff face. An early evening departure is followed by a meal to the accompaniment of Bouzoki music and Greek dancing and a not entirely sober return to Crete after dark. If the company is not too boisterous it makes a memorable and spectacular day excursion from Crete.

Perhaps the most interesting of the vessels in the trade is Minoan Cruises *Artemis*, built in 1960 as the Zeeland Steamship Company's *Koningin Wilhelmina* for the Harwich to

Above: *Minoan Cruise Line's **Artemis** at anchor in the Bay of Thera with her running mate **Minoan Prince** at the harbour beyond on cruises from Crete to the volcanic island of Santorini.*

Below: *Originally Townsend's first **Free Enterprise**, the **Kallisti** of Saronic Cruises at her berth in Heraklion in Crete prior to her daily cruise to Santorini.*

Chapter 19 | *A Final Miscellany*

Although the primary purpose of this book is to consider the ferry vessels in operation in Greek waters, it is appropriate to close with a brief review of more elderly ships which have reached retirement in Greece but have remained in geriatric existence in odd corners of the Greek coast.

The most bizarre of this shadow fleet was the *City of Taranto*, laid-up at Chalkis in the channel separating the mainland from the Island of Evia until sale for scrap in 1998. Last survivor of eleven oil tankers converted for use as ferries between the mid-1960s and mid-1970s, she was a product of Smit Dok in Rotterdam dating from 1953 and originally measured 9,583 tons. Converted at Perama between 1966 and 1968, she became ANEK's first ferry when she entered service as the *Kydon* carrying 860 passengers and 180 cars, loaded through side doors. She saw regular service on ANEK's services from Crete to Piraeus until the mid-1980s, after which she was laid-up and in 1989 sold to investors who bestowed her final rather inappropriate name. Apart from occasional service as an accommodation ship, she did not see further ferry service and was laid-up at Chalkis from 1996. She represented a fascinating period in the Greek ferry business where post-war tonnage, out-dated in its original trades, was converted by the innovative shipyards of Greece to meet needs that could not be supplied by any other segment of the market. Slow and undoubtedly ugly, the converted tankers provided enormous vehicle areas for their time and opened up the way to the carriage of the large lorries which are now a dominant factor in the Greek ferry scene and which have made possible the development of easy and profitable freight transport to and from the Greek Islands.

Of a similar period, and converted at a similar time to meet the same needs, two of Ellerman Line's fast refrigerated cargo vessels on the England to South Africa route also became ferries in Greece and both remained in existence at the time that this book closed for press. The *City of York* and the *City of Exeter* were both built in 1953 by Vickers Armstrong in Newcastle. Rendered obsolete by the spread of containerisation at the end of the 1960s, both were sold out of the rapidly contracting Ellerman fleet in 1971 and were converted in Perama for service with Karageorgis Lines. Their

refrigerated cargo holds became vast garages, again accessed through large side doors. More spectacularly, the whole of the upper works of each ship were cut away so that from a conventional ocean cargo ship of the 1950s there emerged a weird but undoubtedly effective accommodation block and even more peculiar streamlined funnel to a design might easily have originated in a 1930s' American comic book. They operated in tandem with the former Union-Castle liner *Bloemfontein Castle* on Adriatic Services from Patras. Sailing under the names of *Mediterranean Sky* and *Mediterranean Sea* respectively (the Union-Castle ship being *Mediterranean Star*), they provided a profitable and intriguing part of the Greek sea for some fifteen years. On reaching a point where they were quite outclassed by the ferry ships then entering the Adriatic trade they were not replaced and Karageorgis left the ferry market. The *Mediterranean Sea* was renamed *Alice* and spent a considerable period in lay-up at Khalkis alongside the *City of Taranto* but has since been reported sold for breaking up. Her sister ship *Mediterranean Sky* was briefly and unexpectedly brought back for apparent service from Patras but spent much of 1997 and 1998 laid-up alongside the central mole in the port under arrest. By August 1998 she had become an embarrassment to the port authorities and was certainly no ornament to the bustling port at the time she was towed away to continue her lay-up in Elefsis.

SNCF's first car ferry, the *Compiegne* of 1958, was also the first car ferry built in France. Her design was also the inspiration for Hellenic Mediterranean lines *Egnatia*, described in Chapter 10. The railway ship enjoyed what by later standards would be perceived to be a quiet life, her winter including single sailings on alternate days between Calais and Dover, before being withdrawn at the end of the 1980 season and sold initially to Strintzis Lines, for whom she operated as *Ionian Glory* between Patras and Corfu and the Italian port of Brindisi. Replaced by larger vessels she re-appeared under the name *Queen Vergina* and later *Freedom I* and it is under that name that she remains laid-up in Elefsis. Substantially altered her sale to Greece, she is nonetheless recognisable and, even though her future can surely consist only of a final voyage to a scrap yard, the length of lay-up and long expectation of a rise in the value of scrap metal which has characterised Greek ship owners' calculations may see this delayed for many years to come.

While the current ferry fleet of Greece represents one of the most active and innovative collections in the world, the pace of modernisation has meant that there are many elderly vessels seeing out their last days secured to buoys in the anchorages of Elefsis and Khalkis. In many cases radically altered from the shapes and styles under which they were known at earlier stages in their lives, they nonetheless represent a floating museum of almost fifty years of ferry design.

Left: *SNCF's inaugural car ferry* **Compiegne** *was extensively altered when sold to Strintzis Lines in 1980 as their* **Ionian Glory**. *Rapidly replaced by larger tonnage she has since had a peripatetic career, her most recent name being* **Freedom 1** *in which capacity she has served as a refugee ship. Long periods of lay up having included 1995 which she spent at a quay at Perama – radically altered yet easily recognisable as the first car ferry built in France.*

Above: *Externally little altered from her days as P&O Southern Ferries'* **Eagle** *but now a permanent cruise ship, Festival Cruise's The Azur at her berth in Piraeus dressed overall.*

prematurely redundant despite extensive rebuilding and extension of the passenger accommodation in 1976. Both were taken out of service in 1983 and were sold to China but not greatly rebuilt whilst there. In turn replaced on the Hong Kong to Shanghai route by larger tonnage, she came to the Mediterranean and has now served as the *Princess Cypria* for ten years in her current service for which her modest vehicle deck is admirably suited.

The third member of the fleet is the *Princessa Marissa*, built in 1966 as the *Finnhansa*. A large vessel of 7,820 tonnes at the time of her introduction by Finn Lines on their Helsinki to Lubeck service, she was sold in 1978 to Birka Line of Mariehamn and was used as their *Prinsessan* in the day cruise market from Stockholm to Mariehamn until sale in 1987 following the introduction of the *Birka Princess*. Little rebuilt for her trade in the Mediterranean she remains one of the most impressive examples of a mid-1960s Scandinavian ferry still operating in a condition little altered from her original form.

Mediterranean Cruises

Among the host of cruise vessels sailing in the Eastern Mediterranean, two of the more elegant were built as ferries and have maintained their classic lines.

By far the older of the pair, and another survivor from Coast Lines group, is Royal Olympic Lines' *Orpheus*. Built in 1948 at Harland and Wolff in Belfast for the British and Irish Steam Packet Co. as their *Munster*, she generally followed the standard design of motor ships of the Coast Lines group. Operating on the Liverpool to Belfast service until replacement in 1969 she presents a classic profile of a night ferry from the era before the motor vehicle became the dominant factor in coastal shipping. Sold to Epirotiki Cruises, she was elegantly converted with considerable improvement to her profile in Elefsis and has spent over twenty of the intervening years on

charter to Swan's Hellenic Cruises for their culture based voyages for mainly British passengers. Eventually replaced despite immense popularity from her regular customers, she has unexpectedly resumed operations in the merged fleets of Epirotiki and Olympic Cruises. With her grey-green hull, white superstructure and navy funnel she is an elegant reminder of an era of ferry now long gone.

In complete contrast, *The Azur* of Festival Cruises began life in 1971 as General Steam Navigation's final vessel *Eagle*, designed for operation by P&O Southern Ferries on an innovative car ferry service from Southampton to Lisbon and Casablanca. At the time of her delivery one of the largest car ferries in the world, she was also the originator of a series of ships built at the same Dubigeon Normandie shipyard which later included Fred Olsen's *Bolero* and the Silja Line trio of *Svea Corona*, *Wellamo* and *Bore Star*. The first of these also had a spell in Greek cruising as Epirotiki's *Pegasus* before destruction by fire in 1995. The classic design of the ship did not prolong her service in the P&O fleet and after only four years of service she was laid-up in the River Fal and then sold to the French Nouvelle Compagnie des Paquebots as their *Azur*. After sailing for them for 11 years she was chartered to Chandris Cruises in 1987 and rebuilt further in Piraeus. Since 1994 she has been a member of the Festival Cruises Group and continues to sail in the Eastern Mediterranean with Piraeus as her home port. Comparatively little altered externally from her original construction, although with further passenger accommodation constructed within her earlier vehicle space, she is as representative of her era as *Orpheus* is of hers. Both represent the best of Northern European ferry building of their time and both continue to serve with distinction in Greek waters.

Ferry operation in Greece contains much that is weird, wonderful and unexpected but it is always fascinating.

Shipping Books

The author believes this to be the first book published in the United Kingdom on its subject and sources of further information are fairly sparse. For more details of the vessels reference should, of course, be made to Lloyd's Registers – the most reliable source of shipping information down the ages but far from complete in the details given for smaller vessels.

An invaluable source of information is Geoffrey Hamer's admirable *Trip out in Southern Europe* published triennially by the author at 77 St Mary's Grove, London W4 3LW and supported by annual updates. While confining its scope to a list of the operators, their routes and vessels, it is a uniquely convenient source of information.

Also useful are the annual *Guide* and *Designs* volumes and *Fast Ferries* booklets produced by Ship Pax Information of Halmstad in Sweden. The editor Klas Brogen has assembled a substantial collection of information and photographs covering world-wide passenger shipping presented in an accessible format.

Now out of print are the splendidly photographed *Greek Sea Bridges* and *More Greek Ferries* published in Greece in 1994 and 1995 by Katerina and Stanley Sturmey. The research for this book has been able to improve on some of the information contained in those volumes but both can be recommended for the authors' enthusiasm for their subject..

Guides and Timetables

Originally issued in 1991 as *The Mediterranean Ferry Guide*, Frewin Poffley's annual *Greek Island Hopping* published by Thomas Cook is a remarkable publication. Aimed at the many independent travellers to Greece, it combines a light hearted but well researched and factually reliable guide to many of the Greek islands and principal mainland sites with a helpful and practical explanation of the operation of the ferry routes and an attempt at the timetables. Aimed at the intelligent traveller with no prior knowledge of shipping, it presents a highly personal but generally reliable view of how the ferry system can be used to guide a traveller around the wonders of Greece. Its principal draw-back is the long lead time in publication, which makes the almost obsessive level of detail of the timetables impossible to rely upon but the information given is an invaluable general guide to the nature of services and what can be achieved by using them.

Although Greece follows the normal pattern of much of Western Europe in failing to produce a single national timetable to its public transport, it comes far closer than many. The *Greek Travel Pages* is a monthly book now in its 24th year containing extensive listings of hotels and travel agencies and intended particularly for the use by travel agents within Greece. However, it also contains detailed and reliable listings of both international and domestic sea schedules and has the inestimable benefit of regular up-dating. Its draw-back is that it is almost unobtainable to the general public. Whilst available at a current price of 5,000 Greek drachmas including air mail postage from its publishers,

International Publications Ltd, 6 Psylla Street, 10557 Syntagma, Athens, Greece, it is only available for retail sale either at the publisher's first floor offices (close to Syntagma Square, the hub of commercial Athens) and only (sometimes) at one other place. That is at Eleutheradakis Bookshop, Nikis Street, Athens and nowhere else. In the nature of Greece, this admirable publication is matched by an almost identical one *Hellenic Travelling*, published by Info Publications Ltd, 51 Pironos Street, 16341 Athens, Greece and also sold to the public by the publishers but not sold through the retail trade at all.

The National Tourist Organisation of Greece have offices at 4 Conduit Street, London W1R 0DJ and most European capitals and produce an annual booklet described as *Summer Ferry Schedules* which is distributed free of charge. It has the serious drawback that it is produced early in the year and is based on the schedules applying in the previous year and as a result is not a wholly reliable guide for detailed planning of travels in Greek waters.

Maps and Charts

Greece is a notoriously badly mapped country, many of the current maritime charts are based on surveys undertaken in the 1840s, well before modern techniques were developed. It is hoped that the maps included here, which have been specially drawn by Marilyn Gardner will suffice for current purposes.

ACKNOWLEDGEMENTS

Life and travel in Greece require patience above all other qualities. The preparation of this book has taken prodigious quantities of patience, above all from my fiancée Lizette, who has not only had to endure sometimes uncomfortable travelling and much waiting at Greek ports, but has also acted as principal critic and editor in its production. The publication of the book also represents the triumph of patience on the part of the publishers, Miles Cowsill and John Hendy. The author gratefully acknowledges his indebtedness to each of them.

CONCLUSION

No pretence is made that this book can represent the last word on a subject so wide-ranging and which has received so little previous attention from authors. Suggestions for amendment and updating for a future edition will be gratefully received by the author at 17 Kensington Place, London W8 7PT, United Kingdom.

Right: *The distinctive characteristics of the Russian Kometa class of hydrofoil are well illustrated in this scene of **Flying Dolphin XI** smoking her way to Aegina in 1994.*

The Greek Alphabet

*I*n this book the author has attempted to be consistent in transliteration of Greek place names and commonplace words, but complete consistency is made impossible because of the confused derivation of the modern Greek language. While a knowledge of ancient Greek is a useful basic tool to understanding the modern tongue, it is as unreliable to the understanding of the current language as comparison of Anglo-Saxon with modern English idiom would be. A knowledge of at least the 24 letters in the Greek alphabet is extremely helpful in understanding the subject matter of this book, and the following may be of assistance.

Greek pronunciation is complicated by accents and

Above: *Aboard **HML's Egnatia II** on a summer's morning sailing between the islands of Greece's Adriatic coast.*

Greek capital	Greek small	English equivalent	Name	Approximate pronunciation
A	α	A	alpha	*r*at
B	β	B/V	beta	o*v*er
Γ	γ	G/Y	gamma	*s*ugar/*y*es
Δ	δ	D	delta	fa*th*er
E	ε	E	epsilon	b*e*t
Z	ζ	Z	zeta	*z*oo
H	η	E	eta	f*ee*t
Θ	θ	TH	theta	au*th*or
I	ι	I	iota	f*ee*t
K	κ	K	kappa	*sk*in
Λ	λ	L	lamda	*l*eave
M	μ	M	mu	*m*ay
N	ν	N	nu	*n*ot
Ξ	ξ	KS	exi	bo*x*
O	ο	O	omikron	d*o*t
Π	π	P	pi	*p*ick
P	ρ	R	rho	th*r*ee
Σ	σ	S	sigma	*s*ea
T	τ	T	tau	*t*ap
Y	υ	U	upsilon	sh*ee*p
Φ	φ	F/PH	phi	*f*at
X	χ	H/CH	chi	lo*ch*
Ψ	ψ	PS	psi	tap*s*
Ω	ω	O	omega	b*ough*t

diphthongs, many have special values but we can ignore them.

The following vocabulary may assist in an understanding of some of the more common Greek names used in this book.

Greek	English equivalent	Translation
ΑΓΙΑ	Aye-a	Saint (female)
ΑΓΙΟΣ	Aye-os	Saint (male)
ΑΝΟΝΙΜΟΣ ΝΑΥΤΙΚΟΣ ΕΤΑΙΡΕΙΑ	Anonimos Naftikos Etaireia (A.N.E.)	Shipping Company Limited
ΕΠΙΦΑΤΙΚΟΝ	Epifatikon	Passenger ship
ΕΞΠΡΕΣΣ	Express	Not a fast craft
ΚΕΝΤΠΙΚΟ ΓΡΑΦΕΙΟΝ	Kentriko Grapheion	Central Office
ΚΕΡΚΥΡΑ	Kerkyra	Corfu
ΚΟΙΝΟΝ ΤΑΜΕΙΟΝ ΕΙΣΠΡΑΞΕΙΩΝ ΛΕΩΦΟΡΕΙΩΝ	Koinon Tameion Eispraxeion Leoforeion (KTEL)	Joint pool of bus owners
ΚΡΙΤΙ	Kriti	Crete
ΟΧΥΜΑΒΙΤΙΚΟΝ	Okhymavatikon	Vehicle ferry
ΠΑΝΑΓΙΑ	Panagia	The all-holy (female) (i.e. the Virgin Mary)
ΠΑΝΤΟΚΡΑΤΟΡ	Pantokrator	Ruler of All (i.e. Christ)
ΠΡΑΚΤΟΡΕΙΟΝ	Praktoreion	Booking Office

Fleet List

The following list shows the Greek ferry fleet in summer 1999, although in a fast changing environment it will inevitably be overtaken by events. For information on subsequent changes the regular reports in the publishers' magazine 'European Ferry Scene' should be consulted.

The data given represents the most reliable information available and may differ from that published elsewhere, particularly due to the extensive rebuilding often undertaken before a vessel takes up service in Greek waters. Where the available information is not considered reliable a dash (–) has been left in the lists. Not all of the tonnages quoted have yet been re-calculated under the current rules, the exceptions are indicated by an asterisk (*).

The 'flag' column represented the current country of registry of the vessel, however changes of flag on ships engaged in international services occur frequently. The following codes are used:

BE – Belgium	HR – Croatia	TR – Turkey
BZ – Belize	IT – Italy	VG – St Vincent & The Grenadines
CY – Cyprus	MT – Malta	
GR – Greece	PA – Panama	

Name	Flag	Built	Tonnage	Passengers	Cars	Lane Metres	Notes/*Previous Names*
ACCESS FERRIES							
Hermes	CY	1962	*3,783	850	135	198	*Nils Holgersson*
							Mary Poppins
							Samaina
							Nettuno
ADRIATICA							
(only ships scheduled to call in Greece are listed)							
Egitto Express	IT	1974	*8,975	828	221	360	*Espresso Cagliari*
							Espresso Egitto
Laurana	IT	1992	10,977	1,094	272	400	
AGAPITOS LINES							
Golden Vergina	GR	1966	4,555	1,500	170	120	*Corse*
Naias II	GR	1966	6,712	1,541	220	180	*Comte de Nice*
Naias Express	GR	1971	*3,909	1,200	205	326	*Ailsa Princess*
							Earl Harold
							Dimitra
Panagia Ekatontapyliani	GR	1972	*5,590	1,400	217	450	*Hengist, Stena Hengist, Romilda, Apollon Express 2*
Sea Speed 1	GR	1999	605	447	0	0	Catamaran
Super Naias	GR	1972	11,334	1,700	500	675	*Argo*
							Kriti
AGAPITOS EXPRESS (and EXPRESS TRAILERS)							
Express Afrodite	GR	1977	11,850	1,700	336	430	*St Columba*
							Stena Hibernia
							Stena Adventurer
Express Apollon	GR	1973	*5,590	1,432	217	450	*Senlac*
							Apollon Express I
Express Athina	GR	1973	5,643	1,200	212	218	*Prins Philippe*
							Moby Love
							Panagia Tinou II
Express Danae	GR	1972	3,518	852	52	–	*Kyklades*
							Methodia, Express Evoikos
Express Hermes	GR	1968	*3,397	850	180	264	*Princesse Astrid*
							Bari Express
Express Olympia	GR	1973	*4,358	1,200	300	414	*Viking 4*
							Earl Granville
Express Santorini	GR	1974	4,140	1,400	250	350	*Chartres*
Sea Trailer	GR	1973	*7,060	0	0	950	Express Trailers
							Shima Maru
							Ferry Kurushio
AGOUDIMOS							
Kapetan Alexandros A	MT	1962	4.908	1,200	130	315	*Doric Ferry*
							Atlas II
Penelope A	GR	1972	*5,109	1,400	210	450	*Horsa*
							Stena Horsa

Name	Flag	Built	Tonnage	Passengers	Cars	Lane Metres	Notes/*Previous Names*
AMORGOS FERRIES							
Express Paros	GR	1965	*1,369	600	–	–	*Kefolinia*
Syros Express	GR	1970	*1,070	557	–	–	*Aegeus*
							Zephyros
ANATOLIA FERRIES							
Bosporos	VG	1962	4,727	850	105	90	*Koningin Fabiola*
							Lydia
							Bergama
Jupiter	CY	1969	10,524	880	420	1,214	*Surrey*
							Patras
							Anna V
ANEK							
Aptera	GR	1973	8,175	1,550	500	960	*Pegasus*
Candia	GR	1971	*7,291	1,500	350	455	Charter to DANE
							Central No 2
El-Venizelos	GR	1984/92	38,261	3,000	890	1,650	*Stena Polonica, Bonanza*
Kriti I	GR	1979	14,375	870	600	1,700	*New Suzerain*
Kriti II	GR	1979	14,375	870	600	1,700	*New Yukari*
Lato	GR	1975	*15,404	1,564	850	1,200	*Daisetsu*
							Varuna
Lissos	GR	1972	13,407	1,300	556	675	*Ferry Hamanasu*
Rethimnon	GR	1971	*7,291	1,444	350	840	*Central No. 5*
Sophoklis V	GR	1990	*13,384	700	–	1,925	*Hermes*
(ANEK Newbuilding 1)	GR	2000	30,000	1,850	925	1,560	
(ANEK Newbuilding 2)	GR	2001	30,000	1,850	925	1,560	
ARKADIA							
Megistanas	MT	1959	9,940	827	240	525	laid-up Elefsis
							Sassnitz, Silver Paloma
Poseidon Express	GR	1974	*7,824	1,280	220	220	laid-up Elefsis
							Provence
Poseidon Express 2	GR	1973	7,819	1,070	220	400	*Saint Patrick,*
							Saint Colum I
							Dimitrios Express
ARONIS CORFU							
City of Corfu	GR	1953	*491	520	0	0	*Maid of Argyll*
							City of Piraeus
ARSINOI							
Arsinoi	GR	1980	*800	632	–	–	*Anny*
ASCOT LINES							
Thessaloniki	MT	1966	10,499	1,208	247	468	*Prinz Hamlet*
							Kamiros
CATAMARAN FERRY LINES							
Manto	BE	1993	317	192	0	0	Catamaran
CORFU							
Agapitos A	GR	1967	*723	–	–	–	Landing Craft
Agios Dimitrios	GR	1972	*498	–	–	–	Landing Craft
Antonios P	GR	1967	*893	–	–	–	Landing Craft
Dimos P	GR	1975	*864	435	–	–	Landing Craft
Ekaterini P	GR	1975	*841	–	–	–	Landing Craft
Irini	GR	1965	*500	–	–	–	Landing Craft
Kerkyra	GR	1984	*934	–	–	–	Landing Craft
Nanti	GR	1973	*997	–	–	–	Landing Craft
Platytera	GR	1981	*997	–	–	–	Landing Craft
Spyros S II	GR	1977	*622	–	–	–	Landing craft
Tatiana Agapitou II	GR	1969	*788	–	–	–	Landing Craft
Theologos P	GR	1985	*995	–	–	–	Landing Craft
Vivi L	GR	1977	*983	–	–	–	Landing Craft
Xanthoula B	GR	1974	*964	–	–	–	Landing Craft
CRETAN FERRIES							
Arkadi	GR	1983	*6,809	1,500	300	605	*Bizan Maru*
Nearchos	GR	1982	248	200	0	0	Catamaran *Rosario*
Preveli	GR	1980	15,350	604	420	650	*Ferry Orange No 2*

Fleet List

Name	Flag	Built	Tonnage	Passengers	Cars	Lane Metres	Notes/*Previous Names*
DANE							
Candia	GR	1971	*7,291	1,500	350	455	Charter from ANEK *Central No 2*
Ialyssos	GR	1966	8,586	1,243	260	276	*Finnpartner Stena Baltica*
Leros	GR	1968	*5,476	1,400	300	420	Damaged by fire 1998 *Canguro Bruno Ionian Sea, Dimitra*
Patmos	GR	1972	*7,480	1,400	343	990	*Izu No.11*
Rodos	GR	1973	10,298	1,400	400	500	*Argo, Ferry Kogane Maru, Pegasus*
DD FERRIES							
Express Karistos	GR	1971	3,017	600	90	150	*Aetos Dodekanissos Corfu Sea*
DILER LINES							
Captain Zaman I	BZ	1966	12,374	1,200	340	480	*Saga Stena Atlantica Finnpartner Olau Finn Folkliner Festos*
Captain Zaman II	BZ	1966	*7,264	1,532	300	540	*Svea, Hispania Saga ,Knossos*
DODECANESE HYDROFOILS							
Aristea M	GR	1973	135	100	0	0	Hydrofoil *Powiew Maria*
Georgios M	GR	1973	142	100	0	0	Hydrofoil *Poszum Wanda*
Gina	GR	1981	142	116	0	0	Hydrofoil
Gina II	GR	1973	142	100	0	0	Hydrofoil *Kometa 3 Kalina*
Marilena	GR	1981	142	116	0	0	Hydrofoil
Marilena II	GR	1978	142	100	0	0	Hydrofoil *Rodos*
Patmos	GR	1978	142	116	0	0	Hydrofoil
EUBOEA							
Panagia Skiathou	GR	1999	1,500	1,000	120	–	
EUROPEAN SEAWAYS							
Ionis	MT	1977	*2,963	900	200	290	-
FEAX EXPRESS LINES							
Pantokrator	GR	1989	4,296	1,000	170	280	*Superflex Foxtrot*
FIVE STARS LINES							
Poseidon	MT	1970	15,237	1,480	400	650	*Ferry Lilac, Suzuran Maru*
FLYING DOLPHINS							
Flying Cat 1	GR	1990	478	336	0	0	Catamaran
Flying Dolphin I	GR	1975	142	132	0	0	Hydrofoil
Flying Dolphin II	GR	1975	142	132	0	0	Hydrofoil
Flying Dolphin III	GR	1976	142	132	0	0	Hydrofoil
Flying Dolphin IV	GR	1976	142	132	0	0	Hydrofoil
Flying Dolphin V	GR	1976	142	132	0	0	Hydrofoil
Flying Dolphin VI	GR	1976	142	132	0	0	Hydrofoil
Flying Dolphin VII	GR	1976	142	116	0	0	Hydrofoil
Flying Dolphin VIII	GR	1976	142	116	0	0	Hydrofoil
Flying Dolphin IX	GR	1977	142	132	0	0	Hydrofoil
Flying Dolphin X	GR	1978	142	116	0	0	Hydrofoil
Flying Dolphin XII	GR	1979	142	116	0	0	Hydrofoil
Flying Dolphin XIV	GR	1981	142	116	0	0	Hydrofoil
Flying Dolphin XV	GR	1981	142	116	0	0	Hydrofoil
Flying Dolphin XVI	GR	1981	142	116	0	0	Hydrofoil
Flying Dolphin XVII	GR	1985	130	116	0	0	Hydrofoil
Flying Dolphin XVIII	GR	1985	130	155	0	0	Hydrofoil
Flying Dolphin XIX	GR	1985	130	155	0	0	Hydrofoil
Flying Dolphin XX	GR	1975	142	116	0	0	Hydrofoil *Kometa 10*
Flying Dolphin XXI	GR	1976	142	116	0	0	Hydrofoil *Kometa 17*
Flying Dolphin XXII	GR	1977	142	100	0	0	Hydrofoil *Kometa 32*
Flying Dolphin XXIII	GR	1980	142	100	0	0	Hydrofoil *Kometa 43*

Name	Flag	Built	Tonnage	Passengers	Cars	Lane Metres	Notes/*Previous Names*
Flying Dolphin XXIV	GR	1974	127	100	0	0	Hydrofoil *Kometa 23*
Flying Dolphin XXV	GR	1975	127	100	0	0	Hydrofoil *Kometa 26*
Flying Dolphin XXVI	GR	1975	136	100	0	0	Hydrofoil *Kometa 27*
Flying Dolphin XXVII	GR	1975	136	100	0	0	Hydrofoil *Kometa 28*
Flying Dolphin XXVIII	GR	1979	142	100	0	0	Hydrofoil *Kometa 40*
Flying Dolphin 2000	GR	1998	271	516	0	0	Catamaran
Megadolphin XXX	GR	1992	218	210	0	0	Hydrofoil *Alijumbo Messina*
Megadolphin XXXI	GR	1986	220	210	0	0	Hydrofoil *Alijumbo Eoile*
Megadolphin XXXII	GR	1989	172	210	0	0	Hydrofoil *Barracuda*
Newbuilding 1	GR	2000	–	1,050	188	–	Catamaran
Newbuilding 2	GR	2000	–	620	70	–	Catamaran
Newbuilding 3	GR	2000	–	620	70	–	Catamaran

FRAGLINE

Name	Flag	Built	Tonnage	Passengers	Cars	Lane Metres	Notes/*Previous Names*
Ouranos	MT	1967	11,621	992	275	456	*Tor Hollandia* *Ariadne*

GA FERRIES

Name	Flag	Built	Tonnage	Passengers	Cars	Lane Metres	Notes/*Previous Names*
Daliana	GR	1970	*5,815	2,240	350	820	*Ferry Pearl*
Dimitroula	GR	1978	11,779	1,000	330	420	*Verga*
Marina	GR	1971	7,895	1,500	380	780	*Green Ace* *Okudogo 6*
Milena	GR	1970	*5,961	2,100	350	490	*Ferry Gold*
Rodanthi	GR	1974	13,457	2,200	330	630	*Virgo*
Romilda	GR	1974	*5,169	1,200	350	440	*Free Enterprise VIII* *Pride of Canterbury*
[*Gomera Jet*]	GR	1995	4,423	550	160	12	Fast Monohull *Kattegat* *Berlin Express*

GOLDEN FERRIES

Name	Flag	Built	Tonnage	Passengers	Cars	Lane Metres	Notes/*Previous Names*
Maria - Pa	GR	1971	2,227	800	–	–	*La Valletta* *Mistral II*

GOUTOS LINES

Name	Flag	Built	Tonnage	Passengers	Cars	Lane Metres	Notes/*Previous Names*
Myrina Express	GR	1991	1,168	595	100	–	
Papadiamantis II	GR	1973	*1,060	650	80	75	*Georgios P* *Anna L*
Supercat Athina	GR	1998	605	375	0	0	Catamaran *Athina 2004*
Supercat Haroula	GR	1996	1,996	1,412	184	120	Catamaran

HELLENIC MEDITERRANEAN LINES

Name	Flag	Built	Tonnage	Passengers	Cars	Lane Metres	Notes/*Previous Names*
Apollonia II	PA	1964	3,950	861	130	270	laid-up Elefsis *Travemunde* *Europafarjan II* *Corsica Nova*
Egnatia	GR	1960	5,725	1,034	130	144	laid-up Elefsis
Egnatia II	MT	1973	11,481	1,100	290	558	*Aurella* *Saint Patrick II*
Media II	CY	1964	5,440	940	200	300	*Viking I* *Viking Victory* *Sunny Boat* *European Glory* *Neptunia*
Panther	PA	1967	6,008	1,311	230	90	laid-up Elefsis *Ulster Prince* *Lang Hu* *Neptunia*
Poseidonia	CY	1967	6,009	1,274	140	90	laid-up Elefsis *Ulster Queen* *Med Sea*

HERMES HYDROFOILS

Name	Flag	Built	Tonnage	Passengers	Cars	Lane Metres	Notes/*Previous Names*
Iptamenos Hermes I	GR	1974	129	136	0	0	Hydrofoil *Condor 4*
Iptamenos Hermes III	GR	1975	174	180	0	0	Hydrofoil *Condor 5*
Nike I	GR	1972	32	67	0	0	Hydrofoil *Shearwater 3*
Nike II	GR	1973	32	67	0	0	Hydrofoil *Shearwater 4*

Fleet List

Name	Flag	Built	Tonnage	Passengers	Cars	Lane Metres	Notes/Previous Names
HYDRA							
Georgios	GR	1990	3,438	800	160	–	
ILIO LINES							
Delfini III	GR	1971	147	100	0	0	Hydrofoil *Lida*
Delfini IV	GR	1980	142	116	0	0	Hydrofoil *Volna*
Delfini VII	GR	1983	142	100	0	0	Hydrofoil *Kometa 57* *Kapitan Sharkov*
Delfini VIII	GR	1977	142	116	0	0	Hydrofoil *Kometa 42*
Delfini XVII	GR	1981	128	100	0	0	Hydrofoil *Krila Kornata*
Delfini XVIII	GR	1975	142	116	0	0	Hydrofoil *Kometa 4* *Daria*
Delfini XX	GR	1980	142	100	0	0	Hydrofoil *Kometa 46*
Delfini XXI	GR	1991	161	155	0	0	Hydrofoil
Milos Flying I	GR	1981	130	155	0	0	Hydrofoil *Delfini V*
JADROLINIJA							
(Only ships scheduled to call in Greece are listed.)							
Dubrovnik	HR	1979	9,796	1,300	332	468	*Connacht, Duchesse Anne*
Marko Polo	HR	1973	10,154	1,500	270	480	*Peter Wessel, Zeeland*
KERKIRA LINES							
Agios Spiridon	GR	1972	3,994	610	155	290	*Shirahama* *Epirus* *Thira II* *Hellas Express*
LANE							
Ierapetra	GR	1975	*6,135	1,300	400	820	*Green Arch, Okudogo* *No.8, Kydon, Talos*
Vitsentzos Kornaros	GR	1975	9,735	1,200	300	390	*Viking Viscount* *Pride of Winchester*
LEFAKIS							
Eftychia	GR	1974	869	–	–	–	*Maria*
Saronikos	GR	1974	1,126	–	–	–	*Astakos*
LINDOS LINES							
Milos Express	GR	1969	*4,797	2,000	250	–	*Vortigern*
LOUIS CRUISE LINES							
Princesa Amorosa	CY	1957	5,026	327	0	0	*Scottish Coast* *Galaxias*
Princesa Cypria	CY	1968	9,984	730	80	428	*Prinsesse Margarethe* *Lu Jiang*
Princesa Marissa	CY	1966	10,487	884	95	450	*Finnhansa* *Prinsessan*
MARLINES							
Countess M	CY	1967	10,093	850	400	435	*Leopard*
Crown M	CY	1966	11,497	590	350	180	laid-up Elefsis *Jupiter*
Dame M	CY	1972	14,015	1,700	500	750	Charter to Cotunav *Ferry Akashi*
Duchess M	CY	1970	6,576	1,000	230	516	*Wanaka* *Breizh Izel*
MED LINK LINES							
Afrodite II	CY	1968	10,310	760	350	900	*Europic Ferry* *European Freighter*
Agios Andreas	MT	1969	10,179	1,120	300	885	*Australian Trader* HMAS *Jervis Bay*
Maria G	MT	1976	*7,020	845	300	650	*Okudogo 3*
MILILIS LINES							
Karistos	GR	1968	830	400	50	50	*Porto Lafia*

Name	Flag	Built	Tonnage	Passengers	Cars	Lane Metres	Notes/*Previous Names*
MINOAN LINES							
Agia Galini	GR	1973	9,588	12	0	888	*Zea*
							Iris
Aretousa	GR	1995	28,417	1,500	1,000	2,250	
Artemis	GR	1960	6,228	1,200	50	0	Minoan Cruises
							Koningin Wilhemena
							Captain Constantinos
							Panagia Tinou
Daedalus	GR	1973	15,039	1,400	500	880	*Ferry Nishiki Maru*
							View of Nagasaki
El Greco	GR	1972	*9,562	1,050	500	650	*Ferry Atsuta*
Erotokritos	GR	1974	12,888	1,000	800	1,200	*Ishikari*
Fedra	GR	1974	17,879	1,600	470	810	*Peter Pan*
							Robin Hood
Festos Palace	GR	2000	30,000	2,200	1,000	1,560	
Highspeed I	GR	1996	4,735	620	152	160	Catamaran
							Captain George
Ikaros	GR	1997	30,010	1,500	608	2,195	
King Minos	GR	1972	10,164	1,800	500	700	*Erimo Maru*
Knossos Palace	GR	2001	30,000	2,200	1,000	1,560	
Minoan Prince	GR	1973	7,735	850	0	0	Minoan Cruises
							Wakashio Maru
							Apollon
N Kazantzakis	GR	1972	11,174	1,800	500	700	*Shiretoko Maru*
Oceanus	GR	2001	28,000	1,300	1,000	2,000	
Pasiphae	GR	1997	30,010	1,500	608	2,195	
Prometheus	GR	2001	28,000	1,300	1,000	2,000	
MIRAS FERRIES							
Martha	GR	1968	*825	450	70	–	Laid-up
Theseus	GR	1975	*2,353	700	350	500	Laid-up Piraeus
							Dundalk
							St Cybi
MISANO ALTA VELOCITA							
Santa Eleanora	IT	1992	500	234	0	0	SES Catamaran
MYKONOS A.N.E.							
Mykonos II	GR	1972	*2,765	12	0	480	*Sailormark*
							Ro-Ro Anglia
NEL							
Aeolos	GR	2000	6,000	1,000	210	–	Fast Monohull
Agios Rafael	GR	1968	4,421	629	148	492	*Caribbean Venture*
							Golfo Paradiso
Alcaeos	GR	1970	*3,931	1,000	230	432	*Mariella*
Mytilene	GR	1973	9,124	1,735	260	585	*Vega*
Sappho	GR	1966	*6,916	950	250	720	*Spero*
Taxiarches	GR	1976	10,749	700	300	1,050	*Union Hobart*
							Agia Methodia
							Euromantique
Theofilos	GR	1975	19,212	1,560	500	810	*Nils Holgersson*
							Abel Tasman
							Pollux
NOMIKOS							
Anemos	GR	1975	*3,484	1,350	230	450	*Ferry Muroto*
Lemnos	GR	1976	*2,200	654	85	110	
Macedon	GR	1972	*2,001	1,074	150	270	*Ferry Nankai 1*
							Kythnos
Skopelos	GR	1965	*1,588	620	140	216	*Gotlandia*
PARASKEVAS							
Keravnos	GR	1972	195	140	0	0	Catamaran *Salida*
PETRAKIS SHIPPING CO.							
Petrakis	GR	1954	159	200	0	0	HMS *Halsham*
							R.G. *Masters VC*
Petrakis II	GR	1957	159	200	0	0	HMS *Sandringham*
Sotirakis I	GR	1957	159	200	0	0	HMS *Thakeham*
Sotirakis II	GR	1958	159	200	0	0	HMS *Thatcham*

Fleet List

Name	Flag	Built	Tonnage	Passengers	Cars	Lane Metres	Notes/*Previous Names*
POSEIDON LINE							
Sea Harmony II	CY	1977	9,321	1,000	250	450	*Ishikari Maru, Lasithi*
Sea Serenade	MT	1976	8,552	1,200	250	445	*Sorachi Maru*
							Lady Terry
Sea Symphony	MT	1976	*4,972	250	–	885	*Buona Speranza*
							Elefsis
							Sea Sonata
PREVEZA							
Agios Nektarios K	GR	1972	*438	–	–	–	Landing Craft
Nikolaos A	GR	1975	583	–	–	–	Landing Craft
Nikopolis	GR	–	–	–	–	–	Landing Craft
Preveza	GR	1990	493	–	–	–	Landing Craft
Vomas	GR	–	–	–	–	–	Landing Craft
RAINBOW LINES							
Artemis 1	PA	1965	4,217	1,040	126	180	*Prinsessan Desiree*
Jimy							
Niobe 1	PA	1969	5,648	800	192	280	*Transcontainer 1*
Nour I							
RION – ANDIRRION							
Agios Charalambos	GR	1972	456	250	–	–	Landing Craft
Agios Nektarios							
Nafpactou	GR	1974	473	250	–	-	Landing Craft
Anglela	GR	1989	775	–	–	–	Landing Craft
Argonaftis T	GR	1982	766	–	–	–	Landing Craft
Dora P	GR	1974	625	–	–	–	Landing Craft
Georgios K	GR	1977	904	–	–	–	Landing Craft
Georgios P	GR	1974	728	–	–	–	Landing Craft
Iphigenia	GR	1964	718	–	–	–	Landing Craft
Maria P	GR	1979	492	–	–	–	Landing Craft
Nikolaos K	GR	1975	583	–	–	–	Landing Craft
Pol	GR	1974	499	–	–	–	Landing Craft
Poseidon	GR	1974	628	–	–	–	Landing Craft *Neptune*
Schipandas	GR	1973	367	450	–	–	Landing Craft
Sophia P	GR	1985	692	–	–	–	Landing Craft
Themistokles	GR	1968	717	–	–	–	Landing Craft
Theofanis	GR	1975	644	–	–	–	Landing Craft
Victoria	GR	1972	425	300	–	–	Landing Craft
SALAMIS LINES							
Nissos Kypros	CY	1958	9,965	1,100	200	–	*Trelleborg, Homerus*
SAMOS HYDROFOILS							
Samos Flying Dolphin I	GR	1980	142	116	0	0	Hydrofoil *Kometa 46*
							Delfini XX
Samos Flying Dolphin II	GR	1979	128	100	0	0	Hydrofoil *Kapetan*
							Giorgios
SARONIC CRUISES							
Kallisti	GR	1962	2,900	1,400	129	144	*Free Enterprise I*
							Kimolos, Ergina
							Methodia II
SARONIC POSEIDON							
Aegina	GR	1967	870	–	–	–	Landing Craft
Afea	GR	1966	616	–	–	–	Landing Craft
Agios Andreas	GR	1994	629	500	–	–	Landing Craft
Aias	GR	1976	903	–	–	–	Landing Craft
Apostolos P	GR	1967	836	–	–	–	Landing Craft *Marianna*
Hellas	GR	1967	730	–	–	–	Landing Craft
Ioannis II	GR	1964	732	–	–	–	Landing Craft
Miaoulis I	GR	1995	1,197	–	–	–	Landing Craft
Odysseas II	GR	1970	1,284	443	–	–	Landing Craft
							Georgios Diogos
Posidon Hellas	GR	1999	2,100	–	–	–	Landing Craft

Name	Flag	Built	Tonnage	Passengers	Cars	Lane Metres	Notes/*Previous Names*
SEA FALCON LINES							
Falcon I	GR	1977	164	116	0	0	Hydrofoil *Meteor 16*
Falcon II	GR	1977	164	116	0	0	Hydrofoil *Meteor 18*
Falcon III	GR	1977	164	116	0	0	Hydrofoil *Meteor 29*
Falcon IV	GR	1977	164	116	0	0	Hydrofoil *Meteor 35*
SPEED LINES							
Ios Dolphin	GR	1975	142	116	0	0	Hydrofoil *Delfini XVIII*
Santorini Dolphin	GR	1991	161	155	0	0	Hydrofoil *Delfini XXI*
STERN							
Çesme Stern	VG	1964	5,739	600	152	260	Laid-up Bari *Viking II* *Earl William* *Pearl William* *Mar Julia*
STRINTZIS							
Eptanisos	GR	1965	*3,433	1,200	190	288	*Valençay*
Ionian Bridge	CY	1976	16,600	740	650	1,054	*Bass TraderIonian*
Galaxy	GR	1972	17,691	1,600	600	825	*Arkas*
Ionian Island	GR	1973	18,858	1,700	600	825	*Albireo*
Ionian Star	GR	1992	19,308	1,000	900	1,800	Sold 1999 *Via Ligure*
Ionian Sun	GR	1969	7,311	1,380	250	480	*Leinster* *Innisfallen*
Ionian Victory	GR	1974	19,539	1,090	600	1,455	*Sunflower Sapporo*
Kefalonia	GR	1975	*3,924	1,100	260	405	*Venus*
Seajet 1	GR	1995	499	400	0	0	Catamaran
Seajet 2	GR	1998	499	400	0	0	Catamaran *Mirage*
Superferry	MT	1972	14,797	1,400	330	690	Chartered to Swansea-Cork *Izu Maru 3*
Superferry II	GR	1974	*5,052	2,380	271	380	*Prince Laurent*
Superferry Chios	GR	2001	16,500	2,100	420	500	
Superferry Europe 1	GR	2000	20,000	1,600	850	1,780	
Superferry Europe 2	GR	2000	20,000	1,600	850	1,780	
Superferry Hellas	GR	1987	16,725	1,500	116	2,000	*Varuna*
Superferry Ithaki	GR	2000	16,500	1,500	350	500	
Superferry Mykonos	GR	2001	16,500	1,500	350	500	
SUPERFAST FERRIES							
Superfast I	GR	1995	23,663	1,397	830	1,850	
Superfast II	GR	1995	23,663	1,397	830	1,850	
Superfast III	GR	1998	29,067	1,400	830	1,852	
Superfast IV	GR	1998	29,067	1,400	830	1,852	
Superfast V	GR	2000	–	1,500	1,000	–	
Superfast VI	GR	2000	–	1,500	1,000	–	
Superfast VII	GR	2001	–	1,500	1,000	–	
Superfast VIII	GR	2001	–	1,500	1,000	–	
Superfast IX	GR	2002	–	1,500	1,000	–	
Superfast X	GR	2002	–	1,500	1,000	–	
THASSOS A.N.E.							
Thassean Dolphin	GR	1979	128	100	0	0	Hydrofoil *Krila Pirana* *Delfini XV*
Thassos I	GR	1975	1,194	447	–	–	Landing craft
Thassos II	GR	1970	543	446	–	–	Landing craft *Kavala*
Thassos III	GR	1964	225	313	–	–	Landing craft *Antipolis*
Thassos IV	GR	1980	724	620	–	–	Landing craft
Thassos V	GR	1993	832	–	–	–	Landing craft *Avra*
TURKISH MARITIME LINES							

TURKISH MARITIME LINES
(Only ships scheduled to pass the Corinth Canal are listed)

Name	Flag	Built	Tonnage	Passengers	Cars	Lane Metres	Notes/*Previous Names*
Ankara	TR	1983	10,552	983	214	468	
Iskenderun	TR	1991	10,583	800	214	468	
Samsum	TR	1985	10,583	710	214	470	

Name	Flag	Built	Tonnage	Passengers	Cars	Lane Metres	Notes/*Previous Names*
VEFA LINES							
Aulona	MT	1965	5,998	1,100	220	432	*Gustav Vasa*
							Calypso II
VERGINA CRUISE LINE							
Vergina Sky	GR	1971	4,668	1,200	0	0	*Yufu*
							Creta Sky
A.K. VENTOURIS							
Agios Vassilios	PA	1962	4,275	863	135	180	Chartered to Black Sea
							Hansa Express
							Gryf
							Eolos
Arion	GR	1972	11,148	–	–	1,032	Chartered to Sakhalin
							Atlantic Prelude
Euromagique	MT	1977	11,591	350	250	1,589	*Kaprifol*
							Attica
Igoumenitsa Express	PA	1961	5,796	350	150	550	Chartered to Black Sea
							Cerdic Ferry
							Sifnos Express
VENTOURIS FERRIES							
Athens Express	GR	1969	11,003	1,000	300	500	*Brisbane Trader*
Pegasus	GR	1977	8,069	1,300	203	400	*Espresso Venezia*
							Espresso Malta
Polaris	CY	1975	20,326	570	700	2,160	Chartered to Nordo-Link
							Dana Futura
							Skåne Link
Saturnus	CY	1974	8,739	530	250	996	*Scandinavia*
							Europa II
Vega	CY	1975	8,881	500	250	1,044	*Falster*
							Prince de Bretagne
							Europa
Venus	CY	1976	14,540	878	350	1,470	Chartered to St Malo - Cork Ferries
							Dana Gloria
							Dana Hafnia
							Gedser Link
VENTOURIS SEA LINES							
Georgios Express	GR	1965	3,241	* 1,700	190	90	Under arrest Piraeus
							Roi Baudouin
VERGINA FERRIES							
Brindisi	MT	1968	8,326	1,200	320	880	*Ferry Hankyu*
							Raffaello
Valentino	CY	1972	7,593	400	300	900	*Caribbean Progress*
							Aristaos
VIAE SHIPPING							
Nissos Cythera	GR	1975	1,070	* 319	28	100	*Anemoessa*
							Kea Express
							Katerina
ZAKYNTHOS							
Dimitros Miras	GR	1972	2,206	941	20	300	*Olympia*
Ionis	GR	1977	2,963	1,031	92	312	
Proteus	GR	1974	1,160	860	135	–	
Zakynthos I	GR	1973	2,157	680	180	240	*Ville de Corte*

Ancient Greeks – An Earlier Generation of Ferry Ships

Above: *Even in their early days, ANEK competed on similar terms to Minoan Lines, both using converted tankers, the former **Wirakel** emerged as ANEK's first ship the **Kydon** in 1968 and served with them until the late 1980s. She was is seen in 1983 preparing to sail from Piraeus to Chania.*

Left: *For many years an elegant part of the shipping scene between Brindisi, Corfu and Igoumenitsa, the tidy **Roana** was built in 1954 as the **Østersjoen** for service to Bornholm in the Baltic. She came to the Mediterranean in 1973 and remained in service until 1994 and is seen off Corfu.*

Below: *Virtually unrecognisable from her days as Wallasey Corporation's **Royal Daffodil**, the former Mersey vessel was rebuilt to carry a limited amount of vehicle traffic under the names **Ioulis Kea** on the local route to the island of Kea. She is seen loading at Lavrion on an August evening in 1990.*

Above: *Karageorgis Lines operated a remarkable collection of vessels in the Adriatic in the 1970's and 80's including, the* **Mediterranean Star** *whose career had begun in 1950 as the Union-Castle line* **Bloemfontein Castle**. *She is seen on arrival at Patras in 1981.*

Right: *The former DFDS classic ferry,* **Jens Bang** *was launched at the Helsingør shipyard in 1950 for the Copenhagen to Aalborg route. Sold out of service after the 1970 season she spent the following 13 years running between Piraeus, Syros, Tinos and Mykonos. In the colours of Kriton S.A. she was little altered for service in Greece and is seen off Tinos as the* **Naias**, *a name subsequently associated with the Agapitos fleet.*

Below: *The final operating turbine ferry in Europe, Hellenic Mediterranean Line's* **Corinthia** *seen at Patras in 1990 clearly shows her ancestry as British Rail's* **Duke of Argyll**.